THE SPIRIT OF ROMANCE

EZRA POUND

THE SPIRIT
OF
ROMANCE

A NEW DIRECTIONS BOOK

First published by New Directions in 1952.
First published as New Directions Paperbook 266 in 1968.
Manufactured in the United States of America.
Published in Canada by McClelland & Stewart, Ltd.

New Directions Books are published for James Laughlin
by New Directions Publishing Corporation,
333 Sixth Avenue, New York 10014.

FOURTH PRINTING

CONTENTS

PRAEFATIO AD LECTOREM ELECTUM (1910)

This book is not a philological work. Only by courtesy can it be said to be a study in comparative literature.

I am interested in poetry. I have attempted to examine certain forces, elements or qualities which were potent in the mediæval literature of the Latin tongues, and are, I believe, still potent in our own.

The history of an art is the history of masterwork, not of failures, or mediocrity. The omniscient historian would display the masterpieces, their causes and their inter-relation. The study of literature is hero-worship. It is a refinement, or, if you will, a perversion of that primitive religion.

I have floundered somewhat ineffectually through the slough of philology, but I look forward to the time when it will be possible for the lover of poetry to study poetry—even the poetry of recondite times and places—without burdening himself with the rags of morphology, epigraphy, *privatleben* and the kindred delights of the archaeological or " scholarly" mind. I consider it quite as justifiable that a man should wish to study the poetry and nothing but the poetry of a certain period, as that he should study its antiquities, phonetics or paleography and be, at the end of his labours, incapable of discerning a refinement of style or a banality of diction.

There are a number of sciences connected with the study of literature. There is in literature itself the Art, which is not, and never will be, a science.

Art is a fluid moving above or over the minds of men.

Having violated one canon of modern prose by this metaphysical generality, I shall violate another. I shall make a florid and metaphorical comparison.

Art or an art is not unlike a river, in that it is perturbed at times by the quality of the river bed, but is in a way independent of that bed. The color of the water depends upon the substance of the bed and banks immediate and preceding. Stationary objects are reflected, but the quality of motion is of the river.

The scientist is concerned with all of these things, the artist with that which flows.

It is dawn at Jerusalem while midnight hovers above the Pillars of Hercules. All ages are contemporaneous. It is B.C., let us say, in Morocco. The Middle Ages are in Russia.[1] The future stirs already in the minds of the few. This is especially true of literature, where the real time is independent of the apparent, and where many dead men are our grandchildren's contemporaries, while many of our contemporaries have been already gathered into Abraham's bosom, or some more fitting receptacle.

What we need is a literary scholarship, which will weigh Theocritus and Yeats with one balance, and which will judge dull dead men as inexorably as dull writers of today, and will, with equity, give praise to beauty before referring to an almanack.

Art is a joyous thing. Its happiness antedates even Whistler ; apropos of which I would in all seriousness plead for a greater levity, a more befitting levity, in our study of the arts.

Good art never bores one. By that I mean that it is the business of the artist to prevent ennui ; in the literary art, to relieve, refresh, revive the mind of the reader—at reasonable intervals —with some form of ecstasy, by some splendor of thought, some presentation of sheer beauty, some lightning turn of phrase—laughter is no mean ecstasy. Good art begins with an escape from dullness.

The aim of the present work is to instruct. Its ambition is to instruct painlessly.

There is no attempt at historical completeness. The " Grundriss von Grüber " covers somewhat the same period and falls short of completeness. It consists of 21,000 folio pages, and is, needless to say, Tedescan. To this admirable work I cheerfully recommend anyone who has a passion for completeness. Omitting though it does, many of the facts concerning mediaeval literature, it yet contains references to some hundreds of other

[1] 1910.

works wherein the curiosity of the earnest may in some measure be slaked.

As to my fitness or unfitness to attempt this treatise : G. H. Putman tells us that, in the early regulations of the faculty of the University of Paris, this oath is prescribed for professors : " I swear to read and to finish reading within the time set by the statutes, the books and parts of books assigned for my lectures."[2] This law I have, contrary to the custom of literary historians, complied with. My multitudinous mistakes and inaccuracies are mostly my own.

The book treats only of such mediaeval works as still possess an interest other than archaeological for the contemporary reader who is not a specialist. My criticism has consisted in selection rather than in presentation of opinion. Certain portions of the book are in the strictest sense original research. Throughout the book all critical statements are based on a direct study of the texts themselves and not upon commentaries.

My thanks are due to Dr. Wm. P. Shepard of Hamilton College, whose refined and sympathetic scholarship first led me to some knowledge of French, Italian, Spanish and Provençal, and likewise to Padre Jose Maria de Elizondo, for his kindness to me when studying in Spain.

Some stigma will doubtless attach to Mr. Ernest Rhys, at whose instigation the present volume was undertaken. Guilty of collusion, he is in no way responsible for its faults.

Amplissimas ac manu quae transcripsit gratias.

My thanks are due to Messrs. Smith, Elder and Co. for permission to quote from J. A. Symonds' translation of *The Sonnets of Michael Agnolo* ; and to J. M. Dent for permission to quote from the Temple translation of Dante which I have in the main used where there is no indication to the contrary.

London, 1910   E. P.

[2] This meant from four to six books for the Doctors of Law or Medicine Usually one professor had one book on which to lecture.

Continued A.D. 1929 : This does not of necessity indicate that either I or the Doctors wholly understood the matter before us.

POSTSCRIPT (1929)

My first gropings toward the conclusions tabulated in the
preceding notes were published in London in 1910 via the
benevolence of Ernest Rhys. I have no doubt that the work
cd. be greatly improved, but one kind of improvement
wd. falsify at least one of the measurements, the main difference
of outlook being simply that I then knew less and had more
patience. At least part of the subject matter then treated will
not bear my present acids, and the student wanting, and having
a perfect right to know what happened in a given time and
place wd. be no better off than before I made my preliminary
survey.

The reader who does not want this information can regard
a good deal of what follows (Prolegomena) as footnote or
mere proof that I had examined a certain amount of writing
before coming to my conclusions. The detached critic may,
I hope, find at the end of the whole, some signs of coherence,
some proof that I started with a definite intention, and that
what has up to now appeared an aimless picking up of tidbits
has been governed by a plan which became clearer and more
definite as I proceeded.

A good deal of what immediately follows can not be taken
as criticism, but simply as information for those wanting a
shortish account of a period. The mode of the statement, its
idiom or jargon, will have to stand as partial confession of where
I was in the year 1910.

POST-POSTSCRIPT

A fellow named Smith put me on the road which led to the publication of this book — my first published prose work. He was a Philadelphia travel agent whom I had first seen as a boy, in 1898, when my great-aunt Frank had taken us on a grand tour of Europe. I recognized him again by a peculiar movement of his left arm, the elbow had been badly reset, when I was getting off to Europe on my own, after Crawfordsville. With my ticket he gave me a note to a man in London named Sullivan who had something to do with Covent Garden Market. I do not know how, but he persuaded the London Polytechnic to let me give a course of lectures there: The Development of Literature in Southern Europe. These were a very raw summary of things in Rennart's Seminar at the University of Pennsylvania; out of their condensation, this volume. My friend Ernest Rhys persuaded J. M. Dent to publish it in 1910. As far as I remember it elicited no comment from the press. I had not sent the manuscript to any literary figures for their opinion, it was not the practice in those days, besides I could not conveniently have afforded the stamps. Young writers hustled for themselves then and were not subsidized as a matter of course by lovers of Culture and the Fine Arts. Part of the book was republished in the first volume of "Prolegomena" in 1932, but the publishers ("To," Le Beausset, Var, France) were never able to bring out the second volume. A completely revised edition was brought out in England (Peter Owen) and in the States (New Directions) in 1952.

Looking back, and considering, I feel it fitting that this new American reprint be dedicated: "to 'Smith' with thanks."

EZRA POUND

Venice, May, 1968.

I

The word Romance has a definite meaning when applied to
languages derived from the Latin and to the literature written
in these languages. The part of this literature produced during
the Middle Ages is my immediate subject.

For convenience sake, and remembering that such points of
departure are arbitrary, one might date the Middle Ages from
that year early in the Sixth Century when Cassiodorus retired
to the monastery at Vivaria, taking with him the culture of an
age that was over and sealed.

Cassiodorus had seen the end of the Roman Senate, of which
he had been a member. He had held high office under Odoacer
and Theodoric, and had seen the final victory of Belisarius.

To his taste and to Chapter XLVIII of the *regola* of St Benedict.
we may trace much of the inner culture of the Middle Ages.

Concerning daily manual labor : Idleness is the enemy of the soul ;
hence brethren ought at certain seasons to occupy themselves with
manual labor, and again at certain hours in holy reading. Between
Easter and the Kalends of October let them apply themselves to reading
from the fourth to the sixth hour. From the Kalends of October to the
beginning of Lent let them apply themselves to reading until the end
of the third hour, and in these days of Lent let them receive a book
apiece from the library and read it through.

Speaking strictly, the annals of Romance Philology begin
with some treaty oaths signed at Strasburg in A.D. 841. Romance
literature begins with a Provencal " Alba," supposedly of the
Tenth Century. The stanzas of the song have been written
down in Latin, but the refrain remains in the tongue of the
people.

> Dawn appeareth upon the sea,
> from behind the hill,
> The watch passeth, it shineth
> clear amid the shadows.

But before the Romance tongues, Provençal, Italian, Spanish, French, Portuguese, Catalan, Roumanian and Romansch were anything more than ways of speaking Latin somewhat more corruptly than the Roman merchants and legionaries spoke it, there had been in the written Latin itself a foreboding of the spirit which was, in great part, to be characteristic of the literature of the Middle Ages.

This antelucanal glamor of something which is supposed to correspond to the Gothic in architecture is clearly perceptible in the works of Lucius Apuleius.[1] Apuleius was born 125 A.D. in the Roman colony of Madaura in Numidia ; he was educated at Carthage and in Athens, and was a lecturer by profession· His *Metamorphoses* were written between 150 and 155 A.D. Of his other works there survive theological philosophizing : *On the Universe*, *On the God of Socrates*, *On Plato and his Teachings* ; also his *Apologia*, a defence against the charge of practising black magic ; and the *Florida*, a collection of passages from his lectures.

The *Metamorphoses* or the *Golden Ass*, written around an outline found in Lucian, is a picaresque novel, the forerunner of the Archipreste of Hita, Lazarillo de Tormes and the tales of Rabelais.

Apuleius writes in a style not unlike Rabelais, a style that would, they tell us, have offended Tacitus and disgusted Cicero and Quintilian.   Like Dante and Villon, he uses the tongue of the people, i. e. an incult Latin.   The language of the Roman

---

[1] 1929 : I take it this was mere parroting of Mackail.   did not *know* ; but I had to get through my introduction and in general get to and at the subject of the book I was trying to write.   The statement is correct enough and does no injury to the reader.

court was then Greek. The Troubadours, Dante and Apuleius, all attempt to refine or to ornament the common speech.

In seeking to differentiate between Apuleius' style and that of classic Latinity, Adlington, who translated him in 1566, describes it as " such a frank and flourishing a stile as he seemed to have the muses at his will to feed and maintain his pen . . . so darke and high a stile, in so strange and absurd words and in such new invented phrases as he seemed rather to set it forth to shew his magnificincie of prose than to participate his doings to other." In short, he " parleys Euphues."

I have used the term " classic " in connection with Latinity, and am tempted to use the word " romantic " ;   both terms are snares, and one must not be confused by them. The history of literary criticism is largely the history of a vain struggle to find a terminology which will define something. The triumph of literary criticism is that certain of its terms—chiefly those defined by Aristotle—still retain some shreds of meaning.

Certain qualities and certain furnishings are germane to all fine poetry ;   there is no need to call them either classic or romantic.

The sort of vestal asceticism which is called " classic " in drama like Racine's, or verse like Pope's was certainly not ubiquitous in Greek. The following fragment of Sophocles has all the paraphernalia of the " Romantic " school, and something besides.

Stranger, in this land of goodly steeds, thou hast come to earth's fairest home, even to our white Colonus ; where the nightingale, a constant guest, trills her clear note in the covert of green glades, dwelling amid the wine-dark ivy and the God's inviolate bowers, rich in berries and fruit, unvisited by sun, unvexed by wind of any storm, where the reveller Dionysus ever walks the ground, companion of the nymphs that nursed him.

And fed by heavenly dew, the narcissus blooms morn by morn with fair clusters, crown of the great goddesses from of yore ; and the crocus blooms with golden beam. Nor fail the sleepless founts, whence the waters of Cephisus wander, but each day with stainless tide he moveth over the plains of the land's swelling bosom, for the giving of quick increase : nor hath the Muses' quire abhorred this place, nor Aphrodite of the golden rain.[2]

Neither are witches and magical fountains the peculiar hallmark of the " romantic " : the following lines from Ovid are as haunted as anything in Ossian.

> Stat vetus et multos incadua silva per annos.
> Credibile est illi numen inesse luco.
> Fons sacer in medio speluncaque pumice pendens,
> Et latere ex omni dulce querunter aves.

> Ancient the wood stands
>   unhewn for many a season
> It seems some presence dwells
>   within the grove.

The difference is neither of matter nor of paraphernalia. Seeking a distinction in the style, we are nearer to sanity, yet even here we can scarcely do better than borrow an uncorrupted terminology from architecture.   Such terms as " Doric," " Romanesque" and " Gothic" would convey a definite meaning, and would, when applied to style, be difficult of misinterpretation.   When England had a " romantic school " it was said to join " strangeness " with " beauty " ; this also admits a quibble.

Poetry is a sort of inspired mathematics, which gives us equations, not for abstract figures, triangles, spheres, and the like, but equations for the human emotions.   If one have a mind which inclines to magic rather than to science, one will prefer to speak of these equations as spells or incantations ; it sounds more arcane, mysterious, recondite. Speaking generally, the spells or equations of " classic " art invoke the beauty of the normal, and spells of " romantic " art are said to invoke the beauty of the unusual.

----

[2] Jebb's translation of *Oidipous epi Kolonoi*.

I am inclined to doubt Mackail's opinion that this ornate style of the later Empire is related to the "Gothic" quality of mediaeval literature. One might consider Apuleius' floridity a purely oriental quality, analogous to the superficial decorations of Byzantine architecture, as distinct from its underlying structure. This might ultimately bring us to the question of the correspondences of Indian to Gothic art, and we were so the more entoiled. None of these analogies is very satisfactory. The *Golden Ass* is our objective fact.

To find out how these metamorphoses of Apuleius differ from preceding Latin, we may compare them with the metamorphoses of Ovid. Both men write of wonders, and transformations, and of things supernatural.

Ovid—urbane, sceptical, a Roman of the city—writes, not in a florid prose, but in a verse which has the clarity of French scientific prose.

" Convenit esse deos et ergo esse credemus."

" It is convenient to have Gods, and therefore we believe they exist " ; and with all pretence of scientific accuracy he ushers in his gods, demigods, monsters and transformations. His mind, trained to the system of empire, demands the definite. The sceptical age hungers after the definite, after something it can pretend to believe. The marvellous thing is made plausible, the gods are humanized, their annals are written as if copied from a parish register ; their heroes might have been acquaintances of the author's father.

In Crete, in the reign of Minos, to take a definite instance, Daedalus is constructing the first monoplane, and "the boy Icarus laughing, snatches at the feathers which are fluttering in the stray breeze, pokes soft the yellow wax with his thumb, and with his play hinders the wonderful work of his father."

A few lines further on Ovid writes in witness of Daedalus' skill as a mechanic, that observing the backbone of a fish, he had invented the first saw : it might be the incident of Newton and the apple. On the whole there is nothing that need excite our incredulity. The inventor of the saw invents an aeroplane. There is an accident to his son, who disregards his father's flying instructions, and a final jeer from an old rival, Perdix, who has simplified the process of aviation by getting himself changed into a bird. It is told so simply, one hardly remembers to be surprised that Perdix should have become a partridge ; or at most one feels that the accurate Naso has made some slight error in quoting well-established authority, and that we have no strict warrant for assuming that this particular partridge was Daedalus' cousin Perdix.

Turning to Apuleius' Cupid and Psyche, we become conscious of a different atmosphere. This particular tale is put in the mouth of a most suspicious old female ; it is told in a robber's cave to a maiden captive, snatched from the arms of an expectant bridegroom. We are in the era of " once upon a time " ; that of the later writers, who speak of " the Duke Joshua " and " that good Knight Alexander of Macedon," and refer to the *Talmud* as if it were a man : " Master Talmud says."

The mood, the play is everything ; the facts are nothing. Ovid, before Browning, raises the dead and dissects their mental processes ; he walks with the people of myth ; Apuleius, in real life, is confused with his fictitious hero. He keeps up the farce of truth-telling by putting his exaggerated and outrageous tales in the mouths of strangers, who repeat what they have heard from chance acquaintances. The whole book purports to be of the adventures of a certain young traveller. The Cupid and Psyche is the best and longest of the interpolated tales. Thus the old beldame begins :

There dwelt in a certain city a King and Queen who had three very beautiful daughters ; but although the two elder were very beautiful indeed, it was yet thought possible to tell about them with human praises. But to tell the truth, the youngest was so very especially and exquisitely beautiful that her beauty simply could not be expressed or sufficiently praised with the penury of mortal speech.

From which passage it is impossible not to know what kind of story it is going to be. The one hope is that the things "which never were on sea or land" will be more weird and marvellous than any you have yet heard of ; you read, as a child who has listened to ghost stories goes into a dark room ; it is no accurate information about historical things that you seek, it is the thrill which mere reality would never satisfy.

We have already read of a marvellous city in St. John's *Revelation* ; our taste has become Christianized ; our heroine must move through wonderful places : thus Pater's version :

And lo ! a grove of mighty trees, with a fount of water, clear as glass, in the midst ; and hard by the water, a dwelling-place, built not by human hands, but by some divine cunning. One recognized, even at the entering, the delightful hostelry of a God. Golden pillars sustained the roof, arched most curiously in cedar wood and ivory. The walls were hidden under wrought silver ; all tame and woodland creatures leaping forward to the visitor's gaze. Wonderful indeed was the craftsman, divine or half divine, who by the subtlety of his art had breathed so wild a soul into the silver ! The very pavement was distinct with pictures in goodly stones. In the glow of its precious metal the house is its own daylight, having no need of the sun. Well might it seem a place fashioned for the conversation of gods with men !

Then come voices in the air ; voices "unclothed of bodily vesture" ; the harping of invisible harpers, singing ; the musicians invisible, subject to her will ; the invisible Eros, and the wind Zephyrus, who does her bidding.

Later, she is cast out of her paradise for disobedience, and wanders across the earth, and down into the deep of Hell.

Both themes are popular in the Middle Ages. The probable allegory of the tale, with a reversal of sex, is the same as that in the tales of Ywain and Ossian, although these are usually connected with a Diana myth. The invisible harpers and voices in the air might suggest Ariel ; a translation was known to Shakespeare.

But we must look to the style for our distinction between

17

the Latin of Apuleius and classic Latin. Restraint, which drives the master toward intensity and the tyro toward aridity, has been abandoned. The charm of neatness has lost its power ; the barbaric and the Gothic mind alike delight in profusion.[3] If Europe ends at the Pyrenees, the similarity of Apuleius' style to the later Spanish " culturismo " offers opportunity to some literary theorician for investigating the Carthagenian element in literature. Enough here to point out that there was in Latin an " unclassical " style, from which certain qualities in " romance " literature may be derived.

That the hero of Apuleius' book dies in the odor of sanctity would make him only the more acceptable to the Middle Ages. The last part of the *Golden Ass*, which is a huge parody of the mystic rites, would not have offended the patrons of the feast of fools ; although certain more serious Christians did denounce the author as Anti-Christ. Yet it was not from Apuleius, but from Ovid, that the mediaeval tale-tellers took so much of their ornament and inspiration ; and Apuleius is, perhaps, further removed from the earlier writer of metamorphoses than are Crestien de Troyes or Guillaume de Lorris.

About the time when Apuleius was writing his scurrilous, bejewelled prose, there was composed a poem of some eighty odd lines, the *Pervigilium Veneris*,[4] which is interesting for several reasons. It celebrates a Greek feast, which had been transplanted into Italy, and recently revived by Hadrian : the feast of Venus Genetrix, which survived as May Day. The metric is noteworthy, because in it are seen certain tendencies indigenous to the Italian peninsula, which had been long suppressed by the imitation of Greek scansion. The measure is trochaic. That is to say my teacher told me it was trochaic. The term means nothing to the lay reader. The point is that the *metric* of the

---

[3] 1932 : Spanish point of honor, romanticism of 1830, *Crime passionnel*, down to Sardou and the 90's, all date from the barbarian invasion, African and oriental inflow on Mediterranean clarity.

[4] I discount lines 69–74 as the spurious marginalia of some copyist.

Pervigilium probably indicated as great a change of sensibility in its day as the change from Viennese waltzes to jazz may indicate in our own.

> Cras amet qui nunquam amavit
> Quique amavit cras amet.

> Let whoever never loved, love tomorrow,
> Let whoever has loved, love tomorrow.

A new spring, already a spring of songsters,
Spring is born again to the world.
In spring loves are in harmony, the winged mate in springtime,
And the grove unbinds her locks to the mated rains.
Tomorrow beneath the leafage the binder of loves
    will weave green lodges of myrtle boughs,
Tomorrow Dione from her lofty throne gives decree :

> Let whoever never loved, love tomorrow,
> Let whoever has loved, love tomorrow.

Then from the godly blood and the foam of ocean,
Amid two-footed steeds and cerulean cohorts,
Came forth Dione, wave-born from mated rain.

> Let whoever never loved, love tomorrow,
> Let whoever has loved, love tomorrow.

She paints the purpling year with the jewels of flowers.
She strokes the flower-bosoms with the breath of the west wind,
It is she who scatters damp of the gleaming dew, which the
    night wind leaves behind him,
Its trembling tears gleam and are ready to fall.
The hanging, tremulous drops restrained in their falling
Make fairer the blushing shame of the flowers.
Dew which the stars rain down on cloudless nights
Will unbind the peplum, from their dewy breasts at the dawn :
The goddess bids the rose-maids wed at morn,
Made from Love's kisses and from Cypris' blood,
And out of gems, and flames, and the purple of the sun,
That glow which hides within the saffron sheath
Shall dare at morn unbind the single fold.

19

> Let whoever never loved, love tomorrow,
> Let whoever has loved, love tomorrow.

Divine, she bids the nymphs seek out the myrtle grove.

Then the nymphs pray to Diana :

One thing which we pray thee, Virgin Diana,
Let the grove be undefiled with the slaughter of wild things.
Yea, She bids us ask thee if thy strictness might waver,
She wills that thou deign to come—and thou deemest it
    maidbefitting. . . .
Where thou mightest see the gay chorus singing, for three full nights
    amid the herds and wandering through thy glades,
Through the flowery crown of fields, mid the lodges of
    myrtle ;
And the whole night long will be watched out with continuing
    song.

> Dione reigns in the woodland,
> Give place, O Delian Maid.

> Let whoever never loved, love tomorrow,
> Let whoever has loved, love tomorrow.

Divine, she orders that her throne be decked with flowers of
    Hyblis,
She rules and gives the commands, the graces come to her
    calling,
And the flowers, all that the year brings unto Hybla
And more than the vales yield in Hybla and, in Enna the fields.
Maidens of field and forest come with them wandering,
That dwell in hills, fountains and groves.
And here you may see all the herds and flocks amid the broom
    plants ;
She, the divine, bids the songful wings break silence,
The swan clamor drifts hoarse across the pools.
There, in the poplar shade the Tyrrean girl
Cries with musical mouth, so that love seemeth
The cause of her song, rather than sorrow
For the sister ill-wedded.

Yea, hers is the song, and the silence ours !
Ah, when shall mine own spring come ?
When, as a swallow long silent, shall my silence find end ?

> Cras amet qui nunquam amavit
> Quique amavit cras amet

Mackail deftly transfers the final question, and replies that song did not again awake until the Provençal viol aroused it.

II

The Twelfth Century, or, more exactly, that century whose center is the year 1200, has left us two perfect gifts : the church of San Zeno in Verona, and the canzoni of Arnaut Daniel ; by which I would implicate all that is most excellent in the Italian-Romanesque architecture and in Provençal minstrelsy.

While the " minds " of the age were legislating for orderly angles, and reconstructing the laws of God with an extreme precision, the architects were applying the laws of proportion to buildings " meet for the new religion," (or they were simply continuing the use of Byzantine stone forms, lacking the money to incrust the interior with mosaic) and the Troubadours were melting the common tongue and fashioning it into new harmonies depending not upon the alternation of quantities but upon rhyme and accent.

Some temperamental sympathy may prejudice me in favor of this age. The keenly intellectual mysticism of Richard of St. Victor fascinates me, the Romanesque architecture, being the natural evolution from the classic, seems more admirable than the artificially classic modes of the Renaissance. In the forms of Arnaut Daniel's canzoni[1] I find a corresponding excellence, seeing that they satisfy not only the modern ear, gluttonous of rhyme, but also the ear trained to Roman and Hellenic music, to which rhyme seemed and seems a vulgarity.

It is no new thing to rate Daniel among the masters, as one may learn from Dante both in verse and prose.

The opinion has been out of fashion for some five hundred

---

[1] The general reader is referred to a later essay on Arnaut Daniel, which will be included in the forthcoming volume of *Selected Essays*. (Modern Language Review, January, 1909.)

years ; this is chiefly, I trust in charity to the critics, because poets have not been able to read his language, and because the scholars have not known anything about poetry.[2] Dante's poetry so overshadows his work in prose that we are apt to forget that he is numbered with Aristotle and Longinus among the critics.

Dante praises Daniel with a subtle adequacy both in the *De Vulgari Eloquentia* and in Canto 26 of the *Purgatorio*, where having spoken of Guinicelli as " father of me and of others my betters who ever use sweet and delicate rimes of love," he says to him : " Your lovely songs as long as modern use shall last, will make their very ink precious " : and Il Saggio replies, pointing to a spirit before him : " This one whom I point out with my finger was the better craftsman in the mother tongue. He surpassed all verses of love and prose of romances ; let fools talk who believe that that fellow from Limoges (Giraut of Bornelh) excels him. To rumor rather than truth they turn their faces, and thus fix their opinion before paying attention to art or reason. So did many of our fathers with Guittone, with clamor on clamor, ascribing worth to him alone, until the truth conquered with most folk."

The device of praising Daniel by the mouth of Guinicelli is similar to that used in the *Paradiso*, where St. Dominic and St. Francis are complimented in the speech of a Franciscan and a Dominican respectively.

In Dante's *Treatise on the Common Speech* (ii, 2), Daniel is taken as the type of the writers on love. In ii, 6, his " Sols sui qui sai lo sobrafan quem sortz " is cited among the " illustrious canzoni " to be taken as patterns of " this degree of construction which we call the most excellent." Dante mentions him again in ii, 13 " on un-rimed stanzas " and in ii, 10 on the setting of " stanzas " to " odes," writing as follows : " This kind of stanza is used by Arnaut Daniel in almost all his canzoni, and

---

[2] From this general condemnation I would except Dr. W. P. Ker. I do not however, agree with his essay, " Dante, Guido Guinicelli and Arnaut Daniel."

23

THE SPIRIT OF ROMANCE

we have followed him in ours, beginning : " Al poco giorno ed al grand cerchio d'ombra."

Bornelh is mentioned four times in this treatise ; but the first reference is merely on a point of philology, and in the second Bornelh is taken as the type of the singers of righteousness, or "direction of the will," where the competition was certainly not so keen ; Daniel is taken as the type of the singers of love, no slight matter if we consider it in connection with Dante's speech in Canto 24 of the *Purgatorio* where Bonagiunta recognises him as the author of "Donne ch'avete intelletto d'amore," and Dante says of his own work, "I am one who when love inspires me, take note, and I go signifying after what manner he speaks within" ; and the poet from Lucca replies, "O brother, now I see the knot which held back the notary (Jacopo da Lentino) and Guittone (d'Arezzo) and me, keeping us on this side of the sweet new style which I hear : I see well how your pens press close behind the dictator, which of a surety befell not to ours. And he who sets himself to search further has not the sense to see the difference between the styles."

In the *Treatise on the Common Speech*, Bornelh is further cited (ii, 5) on the hendecasyllabic lines, and (ii, 6) "on construction" at the head of the list ; yet, even if Daniel were unmentioned in this treatise, the passage from the *Purgatorio* which I have quoted, would leave us no doubt of Dante's relative respect for him, while the subtlest compliment of all, is that paid at the end of Canto 26, where Arnaut Daniel speaks, not in Italian, but in his own tongue ; an honor paid to no one else in the *Commedia*. The first line of this speech :

Tan m'abelis vostre cortes deman

is reminiscent perhaps of Folquet of Marseilles,

Tan m'abelis l'amoros pensamens

or Sordello's

> Tan m'abelis lo terminis novels.

So pleasureth me your courteous demand
That I nor can nor would conceal it you.
Arnaut am I, who weep and go a-singing.
In thought I see my folly of old days,
Yet see, rejoicing, the day which is before me,
For which I hope and now pray you in that power's name,
Which guideth you unto the summit of the stair,
Be mindful of my grief in good time.

Daniel did not immediately go out of fashion. Petrarch calls him, " gran maestro d'amor[3] who still doth honor to his native land by his fair, fine-wrought speech."

Whether Dante and Petrarch showed a certain not altogether despicable intelligence in this matter, and whether the modern writers on the subject are to be numbered among " gli stolti che quel di lemosi credon ch'avanzi," I leave the reader to judge. [4]

The sum of the charges against Daniel seems to be that he is difficult to read ; but a careful examination of the text shows that this is due not so much to obscurities of style, or to such as are caused by the constraints of complicated form, and exigency of scarce rimes, but mainly to his refusal to use the " journalese " of his day, and to his aversion from an obvious familiar vocabulary. He is not content with conventional phrase, or with words which do not convey his exact meaning ; and his words are therefore harder to find in the dictionaries, more especially as there is no complete or satisfactory Provençal-English, or Provençal-anything, lexicon yet printed.[5]

Daniel's diction and metaphor are occasionally so vivid as to seem harsh in literal translation, but so are Dante's own : as in the first Canto (line 42) of the *Purgatorio*, Cato's " oneste

---

[3] We may render this : " master of chivalric love-lore."

[4] A more mature judgment, or greater familiarity with Provençal idiom might lead one to prefer the limpid simplicity of some of Sordello's verses.

[5] 1909 : Emil Levy later supplied this want. E. P. 1929.

piume," which " honest plumes " must be rendered " feathery beard," if one is to avoid the ridiculous. Such substitutions must be made in nearly all translations ; and very often a Romance or Latin word stands between two English words, or includes them : thus in the *Pervigilium Veneris* " nemus resolvit comam " can scarcely be translated " the grove unbinds its hair " ; yet the Latin phrase is more picturesque than " puts forth its foliage " ; the word *coma* is used for hair, foliage, standing corn, grass, indifferently :—thus in Gaelic " RUN " means " mystery " or " the beloved."

Daniel's poetry is more likely to claim interest than a record of opinions about it. His canzone, which Dante cites among the models of most excellent construction, opens :

> Sols sui qui sai lo sabrafan quem sortz
> Al cor d'amor sofren per sobramar,
> Car mos volers es tant ferms et entiers
> C'anc no s'esduis de cellei ni s'estors
> Cui encubric al prim vezer e puois,
> Qu'ades, ses lieis, dic a lieis cochos motz
> Pois quan la vei non sai tant l'ai que dire.

> Only I know what over-anguish falls
> Upon the love-worn heart through over-love.
> Because of my desire so firm and whole
> Toward her I loved on sight and since alway,
> Which turneth not aside nor wavereth.
> So, far from her, I speak for her mad speech,
> Who near her, for o'er much to speak, am dumb.

The rimes a, b, c, d, e, f, g, are repeated in the same order six times, with a coda : e, f, g, and the original is one of the most musical arrangements of words in sequence to be found. I mean in applying an international standard. Like all fine poetry it can be well judged only when heard spoken, or sung to its own measure ; a great deal of this is true also of the Sestina form invented by Arnaut Daniel, later introduced into Italy by Dante, and into Spain, I believe, by Fernando de Herrera, "el Divino," a form like a thin sheet of flame folding and infolding upon itself.

The first four stanzas and the envoi of the Canzone, begun above, run as follows :—

I

I am the only one who knows the over-anguish which falls to my lot, to the heart of love suffering through over-love ; for my desire is so firm and whole, never turning away or twisting from her, whom I desired at first sight and since, so that now without her I say to her hot words, since when I see her I do not know, having so much, what to say.

II

I am blind for seeing others, deaf for hearing them, for in her alone do I see and hear and marvel ; I am no light, false speaker about this, for the heart willeth her more than the mouth saith ; for I could not travel roads, vales, plains, and hills enough to find in one sole body so many good gifts as God wills to test and set in her.

III

Sooth, have I stood at many a goodly court ; but with her alone do I find worth beyond praising, measure, and sense, and other good matters ; beauty, youth, kind deeds and gracious ways. Courtesy has taught her nobly and led her forth, so that she is broken off from all things displeasing. I think no good thing could turn from her.

IV

No pleasure would be for me brief or short, from her whom I pray that which I hope she please to divine, for never through me shall she know it openly, unless the heart shall speak out his hiddenness : for the Rhone, from the water that swelleth it, hath never such turmoil as doth that torrent which pools itself with love in my heart on seeing her.

VII

I pray that my song weary you not,
For if you wish to grace the sound and the words
Arnaut cares little whom it please or whom offend.

In the fourth stanza the comparison of the heart to the Rhone overflowing with the spring freshets is Dantescan in its vivid and accurate description of the emotion, and in its taking a particular river for comparison ; Dante does not say " where a river pools itself " but, " Dove l'Adige stagna " (" where the Adige pools itself ")

One can form no accurate estimate of Daniel's technical skill in rimes, and more especially in onomatopoeia—making the sound follow the sense or word—save from a study of the original Provençal ; but his vividness and his delicacy may be understood, I think, from the canzon which Dante praises in the *De Vulgari Eloquentia* (II, 2).

> L'aura amara
> Fals bruoills brancutz
> Clarzir
> Quel doutz espeissa ab fuoills,
> Els letz
> Becs
> Dels auzels ramencs
> Ten balps e mutz,
> Pars
> E non pars ,
> Per qu' eu m' esfortz
> De far e dir
> Plazers
> A mains per liei
> Que m'a virat bas d'aut,
> Don tem morir
> Sils afans no m'asoma.

This verse form, with a sound that echoes the angry chatter of the birds in autumn, is repeated six times with exact repetition of the rimes.

I

> The bitter air strips clear the forked boughs,
> Which softer winds had covered thick with leaves,
> And holdeth dumb and stuttering the birds' glad mouths
> Amid the boughs, mates and unmated all.

Wherefore I struggle to speak and to do more often such things as please her who hath cast me down from on high, of whom I fear to die unless she ease my pain.

II

So clear was my first light in choosing her whose eyes my heart feareth that I praise not the secret delights of another, nor gifts, nor prayers. Nay, my prayer draws itself far away from any other, but my delight is to attend closely to her will, to her good words that never weary one ; hers who so delights me that I am all for serving her, from my feet to my hair.

III

Beware, love,
Consider, if I be truly welcome ?

For if I am unwelcome, I fear to make heard words so mad that it were better you cut short my speech ; for I am a faithful lover, dear, without variance, though many a time you rigorously make me hide my heart, yet with all the snow (in the world) I should have need of a kiss to cool my hot heart, which no other balm avails.

IV

If she will but reach out her hand to me in favor, she who has easily set her power upon me—she who is, as it were, the citadel of worth—out of the silent prayers which I have arrayed within me, will my clear thought be rendered up intact ; for I would be dead did she not make me to suffer hope, wherefore I pray her that she cut short my (time of) hoping, and in this wise retain me gay and joyous, for the joy of re-joicing in anything else I count not worth an apple.

V

Sweet one ! Dear one !

Thou who art the desire of every grace (*i.e.* each of the pure essences wishes her to be its symbol, its means of manifestation), for many a proud, mad deed shall I suffer on your account, for you are the province of all my madness, whereof there is clamour in many a place, but jests (scandal) will not make me turn from you, nor will possessions make me depart. Never have I loved anything so much and with less boasting and I desire you more than doth God her of Doma [our Lady of Dome ?]

VI

(Envoi to the Jongleur)

Now make ready the song and its accompaniment so as to present it to the king, who shall be its target, for reward (of worth) which is blind here, is doubled there, and the customs of largesse and banqueting are kept up. With joy repair thou thither, for if he would award me his ring, never a day would I stay from Aragon, but I should wish to go there galloping—only they have begged me to remain here.[6]

VII

Made is the pact that in my heart I will every evening look again upon her to whom I, Arnaut, render lady service, in which she has neither sharer nor rival, for I am clean done with troubling my head about any other.

In this song, which the greatest of poets has praised, even though it is stripped bare of all beauties of form and of word melody by translation, one can still follow the shadowy suggestion of mediaeval ceremonies, due to Daniel's choice of verbs ; and the symmetrical arrangement of stanzas. The excellence of its construction may, I think, be understood by anyone who will sing the given stanza aloud. *Letz, becs, mutz,* are, it is true, " shaggy " rime words ; but if the ear is to carry seventeen rimes at once, some of them must be acute sounds. Dr. Ker's objection that the harmony of this song is not obtained by the rules of thumb which Dante prescribes for obtaining harmony in another language, does not seem to me valid.

In Canto 26 of the *Purgatorio* Dante's Provençal lines which do not rime with other lines in Italian, contain only ten syllables. And the single line—

Ai fals ris ! per qua traiz avetz

[6] Original text uncertain.

with which he begins the " desacoart," usually styled Canzone
XXI, should show that either 't's and 'z's had in Provençal a
different sound from that which is usually imagined, or that
Dante believed certain things to be fitting in the *lingua materna*
which were not laudable in *lingua Toscana*.

In Stanza I Arnaut speaks of the season ; in most Provençal
poetry one finds nature in its proper place, i.e. as a background
to the action, an interpretation of the mood ; an equation, in
other terms, or a " metaphor by sympathy " for the mood of the
poem. In half Arnaut's songs, and I should think in half the
Provençal canzoni, the first verse sets the stage, and determines
the tone of the poem directly or by inversion.

In Stanza II he speaks of the lady.
Stanza III is a direct appeal to her.
Stanza IV is spoken as if she were to overhear it.
Stanza V is again a direct appeal.
Stanza VI is the conventional address to the Jongleur.

The addresses to the Jongleur, later to be replaced by tornate
or envois addressed to the song itself, often form no part of the
poem proper, and concern only the people of the time, for
which reason, coupled with our ignorance of the personal
circumstances to which they refer, they are often unintelligible
not only in Daniel but in the other troubadours.

The boldness of the comparison at the end of Stanza V is
such that no translation can diminish it. Its arrogance may well
have delighted the man who summoned the rulers of the third
heaven to listen to a poem :

> Voi che intendendo il terzo ciel movete.
> (Il Convito, ii.)

The second canzon to which Dante refers is " Sols sui qui
sai la sobrafan quem sortz," above noted. Four stanzas of the
third,

Sim fos amors de joi donar tant larga
Cum ieu vas lieis d'aver fin cor e franc,

run as follows :

I

Had love such largesse giving joy to me, as I, in having for her a fine and open heart, never, for the great good which I seek, would he trouble to set me hindrance, for now I have set my love in such a high place that the thought exalts and abaseth me. But when I consider how she is the summit of worth, much do I love myself the more for having ever dared to desire her, for now do I know that my heart and my wit will make me to make to their whim a rich conquest.

II

Therefore a long delay will not put me off, for I have set myself toward so rich a place, and " pooled " myself about it ; that with her sweet words alone she would hold me bountied with joy, and I would follow her until they carry me to the tomb, for I am never one that leaves gold for lead ; and since in her there is nothing that one could refine, so will I be true and obedient to her until out of her love, if it please her, she " invest " me with a kiss.

III

A good delay brings back and frees me from a sweet desire whereof my body grieveth me, and in calmness I bear the anguish and suffering and neglect and penury, since, as regards beauty, the other women are in the valley ; for the noblest, whoever she may be, appears as if she had fallen, if she come to be compared with her (my Lady) : and this is true, for every good charm, worth, wisdom and wit reign in her in such wise that there is not one that is there in scant quantity, nor which doth not abide (in her) constantly.

IV

And since she is of such worth, do not think that my firm will can disperse itself or flow away or divide, for by that God who manifested himself in the dove, I am neither mine (i.e. sane) nor hers if I leave her. For the world has in it no man of whatever name so desirous to have great prosperity as I have to be made hers, and I care not a bean for the bores to whom the harm of love is a " fiesta."

32

The second stanza is of the major importance, and those who are trying to trace the sources of Dante's style would do well to consider how much he owes to Daniel's terse vigor of suggestion. Three times in this stanza the Provençal makes his picture, neither by simile nor by metaphor, but in the language beyond metaphor, by the use of the picturesque verb with an exact meaning. Firstly, "pools himself"—the natural picture. Secondly, after the comparison of gold and lead, the metal worker's shop gives tribute, and is present to the vision in the technical word "refine." Thirdly, the feudal ceremony and the suggestion of its pageantry are in the verb "invest."

It was not in a fit of senseless enthusiasm, nor yet because of lost narrative poems of uncertain existence, that Dante praised "il miglior fabbro," but for maestria.

Perhaps the most beautiful of all the surviving poems of "the better craftsman" is the XIIth (according to Cannello's numbering: at least it seems to lose less of its glamor in translation.

Doutz brais e critz.

I

Sweet clamor, cries, and lays and songs and vows do I hear of the birds, who in their Latin make prayers each to his mate, even as we here to those loved ladies whom our thoughts intend; and therefore I, who have set my thought upon the noblest, should make a chançon of fine workmanship above all the rest, where there be not a false word or a rhyme strained.

II

I was not tortured nor taken with fears when first I entered into that castle behind its barriers, there where dwells my lady, of whom I have great hunger such as never had the nephew of St William. A thousand times a day I yawn and stretch[7] because of that fair who surpasseth all others even as true joy surpasseth ire and fury [rampa].

[7] I give the most vigorous and perhaps brutal, though exact equivalent of two words which the euphuist would render " languish " and " yearn."

III

Well was I welcomed and my words attended, so that I was not wrong in choosing her, but I wished rather to take the gold than a twig, that day when I and my lady kissed, and she made me a shield of her fair dark blue mantle, so that the false tale-bearers should not see us ; the tale-bearers with their cobra's tongues, whence so many ill words are set abroad.

IV

May God, the Chosen, by whom were absolved the sins of the blind Longinus, wish if it please him, that I and my lady lie within one chamber where we shall make a rich covenant, whereon great joy attendeth ; where, with laughter and caresses, she shall disclose to me her fair body, with the glamor of the lamplight about it. [*E quel remir contral lums de la lampa.*]

V

The flowering bough with the flowerets in bud, which the birds make tremble with their beaks, was never more fresh (than she) ; wherefore I would not wish to have Rome without her, nor all Jerusalem, but altogether, with hands joined I render me to her, for in loving her the king from beyond Dover would have honor, or he to whom are Estela and Pampeluna.

The last line of the fourth stanza may be taken to differentiate Arnaut Daniel from all other poets of Provence.[8]

Y dar nueva lumbre las armas y hierros.

Literally,

And the arms irons give forth new (or strange) reflections.

The delicacy, the absolute sense of beauty which could beget this line may justify praise even from a man who sang,

[8]There is in the *Muerte del Conde de Niebla* of Juan de Mena (Cordovan, died in 1456) a line strangely different, yet oddly akin to this line of Daniel's. Mena, in enumerating the evil omens which attend the Count's embarkation, does not mention the appearance of the water, but suggests it in speaking of the sullen glow in the armor.

> Tu, nuvoletta, in forma piu che umana
> Foco mettesti dentro alla mia mente,

before he sang of Paradise.

In the VIIIth Canzon there is a bit of technique as beautiful as it is clever :

> High and low among the first come leaves, the boughs and sprays are new with flowers, and no bird holds mute a mouth or throat, but cries and sings,

> > cadahus
> > en son us

each one in his fashion. For the joy I have of them and of the season I would sing, but love assails me, and sets the words and song in accord.

This means, I think, not merely " in harmony with each other," but " sets them in accord with himself " ; though it is possible that I here read into the Provençal more than it actually says, having in my mind *Purgatorio* Canto 24, line 52.

> Io mi son un che, quando amor mi spira, noto, ed a quel modo che ditta dentro, vo significando.

> I am, within myself, one who, when love breathes into me, take note, and go making manifest after what manner he speaketh.

The imitation of the bird note, " cadahus, en son us " continues through the remaining stanzas.

Thus II :

> > Er va sus,
> > Qui qu'n mus,

and III :

> > Mas pel us
> > Estauc clus.

Of Daniel's eighteen extant poems one is a satire too rank for the modern palate ; three begin with a stanza of spring ; one of April ; one of May or June ; one of fruit time ; two of autumn ; one of winter. The rest are of love without preface, except the rhyme of the Uncle and the Nail, " L'Oncle et l'ongla," which is bad enough to have been his first experiment with the sestina, and is, unfortunately, the only one which survives :

The IVth ode opens :

When the ice is gone and over and remains not on hill nor in hollow, and in the garden the flowers tremble on the " between the tips " where the fruit comes, the flowers and the songs and the clear piping and the quaint, sweet season bid me clap my hands with joy, here at the time of April's coming in.

The Vth :

When I see leaf and flower and fruit appear in the twigs of the trees, and hear the song and clamor which the frogs make in the rill and the birds in the wood, then love puts forth leaf and flower and fruit in my heart, so gently that he steals the night from me when other folk sleep and rest and take pleasure.

Perhaps such stanzas may suggest by what process the Plantagenet canzo was, in a less pliable language, transmuted into the shorter Elizabethan lyric forms. For such suggestions in the metric one must examine the texts themselves.

The Xth canzo is notable for the passage :

I have heard and had said a thousand masses for her, and burnt lights of wax and oil, so that God might give me good issue concerning her, with whom no fencing (skill) avails me ;

and for the three lines by which Daniel is most commonly known :

Ieu sui Arnaut qu'amas l'aura
E chatz le lebre ab lo bou
E nadi contra suberna.

I am Arnaut who loves the wind,
And chases the hare with the ox,
And swims against the torrent.

These seem to have become a by-word not only in Provence, but among the moderns.

The monk of Montaldon in a satire alludes to them, not in contempt, as is sometimes assumed, but complaining that Arnaut had written nothing important since the time of their composition ; and Daniel himself, in some later canzos, laughs at them more or less affectionately, but in a way which shows that they had been current in jest and discussion. A copyist's error in writing the first line " Q'amas Laura " gives us an early example of a pun over-familiar to the reader of Petrarch, but the Provençal joke had its source in the second line,

> And chases the hare with the ox.

A good deal of time was wasted on a quibble as to whether the metaphor was permissible. Dante's

> Ieu sui Arnaut qui plor e vau cantan,
>
> I am Arnaut who weep and go a-singing,

is, I should think, designedly reminiscent, and intended to draw attention to the more important qualities of Daniel's art : to which qualities one can scarcely give too much heed, and to the praise of which, seeing that Dante has praised them to the full, it is scarcely possible to add.

To form a relative, critical estimate of this poet, and to calculate how much he loses in translation, consider the line

> Al brieu brisaral temps braus,

noting how unmistakably the mere sound suggests the " harsh north-windish time," of the song ; and then consider what some of our finest Elizabethan lyrics would be if re-written in unmeasured prose.

The excellences whereby Daniel surpasses the other troubadours are not easy to demonstrate in translation. But I think

it is safe to say that he was the first to realize fully that the music
of rhymes depends upon their arrangement, not on their multi-
plicity. Out of this perception he elaborated a form of canzone
where stanza answers to stanza not boisterously, but with a
subtle persistent echo.

His mastery of rhythm is not confined to the movements
of these more stately forms, but extends also to the more jovial
or jazzy lyric measures, as can be seen by :—

> Can chai la fueilla
> Dels ausors entrecims,
> El freitz s'ergueilla
> Don sechal vais' el vims,
> Dels dous refrims
> Vei sordezir la brueilla
> Mas ieu soi prims
> D'amor, qui que s'en tueilla.

Daniel is also to be praised because, through his most complex
and difficult forms the words run often with an unperturbed
order, almost that of prose.

In attempting to decide whether or not Daniel's metrical
practice conforms to Dante's recommendations, one must consider carefully two passages in the *De Vulgari Eloquentia* [II, 7,
40], where Dante speaks of trisyllabic or almost trisyllabic
words—

> vel vicinissima trisyllabitati

and [II, 5, 26 seq.,] where

> Ara auziretz encabalitz chantars

is considered as hendecasyllabic.

> nam duae consonantes extremae non sunt de syllaba praecedente.

III

The culture of Provence finds perhaps its finest expression in the works of Arnaut Daniel. Whatever the folk element in Provençal poetry may have been, it has left scant traces. (What now strikes me [1929] is that Guillaume de Poitiers is the most " modern " of the troubadours. For any of the later Provençals, i.e. the highbrows, we have to make a number of intellectual transpositions, we have to " put ourselves into the Twelfth Century " etc. Guillaume, writing a century earlier, is just as much of our age as of his own. I think it quite likely that all sorts of free forms and doggerel existed and that nobody thought it worth while to write them down. Guillaume being a great prince, snobism took note even of his spontaneity.) The poetry, as a whole, is the poetry of a democratic aristocracy, which swept into itself, or drew about it, every man with wit or a voice. The notable exceptions are the dance songs, for there is nothing to prevent our acceptance of such catches as

> Quant lo gilos era fora
> bel ami
> Vene vos a mi,

or *La Regine Avrillouse* " as songs actually sung by the people at out-of-door festivities (i.e. if we have a folk bee in our bonnets).

" The April-like Queen," or songs of like character, may have been used in connection with such fragments of the worship of Flora and Venus as survived in the spring merrymakings : the dance itself is clearly discernible in its verbal rhythm.

> Al entrada del tens clar—eya !
> Per ioie renovelar—eya.
> E pir jalous irritar
> Vuel la regina demonstrar—eya,
> Qu'el' e si amorouse.

Refrain :

> A la vi, a la vi jalous
> Lassaz nos, lassaz nos
> Baillar entre nos.[1]

There is in the verbal movement no suggestion of the beautiful flowing of garments which Catullus had presumably in mind when he wrote

> Dianae sumus in fide
> Puellae et pueri integri.

But we are hardly fair in comparing *La Regine Avrillouse* to the Latin verse, which follows the classic dance of worship. Our quasi-Zarabondilla, or Tarantella, is the successor, one supposes, of the Cordax of the later Empire. At the time of *La Regina Avrillouse*, the worshippers of Diana, and the Star of the Sea, are moving to the still graver music in cloisters.

The Alba is debatable ground ; the earliest known Alba is in Latin, with five classical names in nine lines of verse ; but the Provençal burden may have been taken from some purely popular song.

The fragment beginning " Quan lo rossinhols escria " may easily be popular. It runs :

When the nightingale cries to his mate, night and day, I am with my fair mistress amidst the flowers, until the watchman from the tower

---

[1] Curiously enough the notation of one melody found with these words does not seem able to support the full vigor of their movement. At any rate when working with Walter Rummel a few years after writing the above we were unable to get a musical interpretation having the same force. (Vide " Hesternae Rosae " in *Neuf Chansons de Troubadours* ; W. M. Rummel, Augner, Max Eschig, Boston Music Co. 1912.) In another ten years I may have found the solution.

cries " Lover, arise, for I see the white light of the dawn, and the clear
day."

The finest Alba, that which begins " En un vergier sotz
fueilla d'albespi," though anonymous, may be either of the
court or of the people. But the friend is " *cortes*," courteous, or
courtly.

The first troubadour honorably mentioned is of courtly rank :
William IX, Count of Poitiers (1086–1127), a great crusader,
and most puissant prince, who belongs rather in one of Mr. Hew-
lett's novels than in a literary chronicle : his fame rests rather
upon deeds than upon the eight poems that have survived him.

The first great " finder " was of lower station ; the *razo*,
or prose preface, says of him :

Bernart of Ventadorn (1148–95) was of Limousin, of the Castle
of Ventadorn, and was one of low degree, son, to wit of a serving-man
who gathered brushwood for the heating of the oven wherein was
baked the castle bread.

Becoming a " fair man and skilled," and knowing how to
make poetry, and being courteous and learned, he is honored
by the Viscount of Ventadorn ; makes songs to the Countess ;
makes one or two songs too many to the Countess ; with the
sequel of a Countess under lock and key, and one more troubadour wandering from court to court, and ending his days at
the monastery of Dalon.

Sic dixit Hugh of St. Circ, as the son of the aforementioned
Countess of Ventadorn, told it him. The best known of Ventadorn's songs runs as follows :

> Quant ieu vey la' lauzeta mover
> De joi sas alas contral ray.

When I see the lark a-moving
For joy his wings against the sunlight,
Who forgets himself and lets himself fall
For the sweetness which goes into his heart ;
Ai ! what great envy comes unto me for him whom I see so rejoicing !

I marvel that my heart melts not for desiring.
Alas ! I thought I knew so much
Of Love, and I know so little of it, for I cannot
Hold myself from loving
Her from whom I shall never have anything toward.
She hath all my heart from me, and she hath from me all my wit
And myself and all that is mine.
And when she took it from me she left me naught
Save desiring and a yearning heart.

I had no power over myself nor have had ever, since it let me see in her eyes a mirror that much pleased me.

O mirror, since I mirrored myself in thee, deep sighs have slain me, for I have lost myself, as Narcissus lost himself in the fount.

I despair of ladies and will trust me to them no more, for, ever as I was wont to champion them, so now I dis-champion them, since I see that one does not hold me in grace. As for them that destroy and confound me, I fear them all and mistrust them, for well do I know what sort they are.

All this makes my lady seem a good woman, wherefore I upbraid her, for I do not wish what one should wish, and I do that which one should.

I am fallen into ill favour, and indeed I have behaved like the fool on the bridge,[2] and I do not know why it happened to me, except that I climb the mount too far.

Grace is indeed lost, and I will never taste it again, for she who should have most of it, never has it ; Where shall I seek it ?

Ah ! how cruel it will seem to whomso sees her, that she let this desirous wretch, who will never have peace without her, die, and aided him not.

At this time (1140-70) lived Jaufre Rudel, Prince of Blaia, whose love for the Countess of Tripoli has been re-sung by so many. The song he himself made runs as follows :

> Lan quand li iorn son lonc en mai
> M'es bels douz chans d'auzels de lonh.

---

[2] Probably an allusion to the fable of the greedy dog, from Æsop.

When the days are long in May
Fair to me are the songs of birds afar.
And when I am parted from her
I remember me of a love afar,
And I go with a mind gloomy and so bowed down
That no song or white thorn flower
Pleases me more than the winter's cold.

Never more will I take joy of love
Unless it be of this love afar,
For a nobler and fairer I know not of
In any place either near or far.

So true and fine is her worth, that on her account I would
I were proclaimed captive there in the realm of the Saracens.

Sooth it would seem as joy, when I should seek, for love of
God, an hospice afar ; and if it please her, I would lodge near
to her, though I be from afar. There would there be faithful
speaking together, when the far-come lover should be so close
that he might have his solace of fair speaking.

I depart wrathful and joyous when I see this love afar ; for
I see her not in the body, for our lands are set apart too far.
Many's the step and the road between us, though for all that
I am not divided from her ; but all shall be as it pleaseth God.

I have true faith in God, whereby I shall see this love afar.
But for one good that falleth to me thereby I have two
griefs, for she is removed from me so far.

Ai ! for I would be a pilgrim thither if only my staff and my
cloak might be mirrored in her fair eyes.

God, who hast made all things that come and go,
And hast fashioned me out this love afar,
Give me power, such as I have not in my heart,
So that in short space I shall see this love afar,
Verily and in a place set to our need,
Be it room or garden it will alway seem to me a palace.

He speaketh sooth who calls me covetous
And desirous of this my love afar, for no other joy
    would delight me so greatly, as the enjoyment of my
    love afar.
But she whom I desire is so hostile to me !
Thus hath my destiny bewitched me to love and be unloved.

But she whom I love is so against me !
May the weird be utterly cursed that hath fated me to love and not be
    loved.

There is a less quoted song of Rudel's which begins :

When the rill frees it from the fount and when the eglantine flower
appears and the nightingale on the bough trills and refrains, and lowers
his sweet song and phrases it, is it right that I should make refrain for
my love in a land afar.

At this time lived also Peire d'Auvergne, of whom Dante
speaks[3] as using that Langue d'Oc which is a more finished
and sweeter language for poetry than the Langue d'Oil ; also
Guillaume of Cabestang, whose heart his lady ate after he was
dead, not knowing what she did, nor that her husband had
slain him through jealousy, and contrived the trick,[4] and Arnaut
of Marvoil who sang of one lady only—so far as we know
from the philologists. A little while after came the other two
who form with Daniel the great triad mentioned in *De Vulgari
Eloquentia* (11, 2) : Giraut of Bornelh and Bertrans de Born.
    The headless trunk which Dante meets in Malebolge is not
more arresting to the attention than the fierce words of the
chastelan of Aultaforte—" lover of strife for strife's sake"—
who sang of his Lady Battle, as St. Francis of Poverty, or the
gentler rimers of " those ladies whom their thoughts attend."
    Dante, remaining to watch the dismal herd, Malatesta de

<hr />

[3] *De Vulgari Eloquentia*, i, 10.
[4] Monsieur Langfors has treated this tradition in an, alas, all too scholarly
manner. A. de Langfors : G. de Cabestanh, Champion, Paris, 1924.

Rimini, Guido of Fano, Fra Dolcino, Mosca, sowers of discord, says[5] :

Certainly I saw, and to this hour I seem to see, a trunk going headless, even as went the others of that dismal throng, and it held the severed head by the hair, swinging in his hand like a lantern, which looking upon us, said, "Ah me !"

Of itself it made itself a lamp, and they were two in one and one in two (He who governeth the universe knows how this can be).

When he was just at the foot of the bridge, it raised its arm with the face full towards us, to bring near its words, which were ; Behold the pain grievous, thou who, breathing goest looking upon the dead ; see if there be pain great as this is, and that thou may'st bear tidings of me, know me, Bertrans de Born ; who gave never comfort to the young king. I made the father and the son rebels between them ; Achitophel made not more of Absalom and David by his ill-wandering goads. Because I have sundered persons so joined (in kinship), I bear my brain parted, *Lasso* ! from its beginning, which is this torse. Thus is the counterpass observed in me.

From this passage in the Inferno most people gain their first impression of Bertrand who from temperament or from military necessity (as I have elsewhere indicated) set the strife between friends and relations, who called the Count of Brittany, father of Shakespeare's tragic young prince, " Rassa," and the King of England " Yea and Nay," and the young king, his son, " Sailor." He has left us one of the noblest laments or " planh " in the Provençal, for young prince Henry.

Yet it is not for this lament nor yet for his love songs that he is most remembered, but for the goad of his tongue, and for his scorn of sloth, peace, cowardice, and the barons of Provence. Thus :

A Perigord pres del muralh,

> At Perigord near to the wall,
> Aye, within a mace throw of it,
> I will come armed upon Baiart, and if I find there
> that fat-bellied Poitevin,
> He shall see how my steel cuts.

[5] *Inferno*, Canto XXVIII.

For upon the field I will make a bran-mash of his brains, mixed with the *maille*[6] of his armor.

Earlier in the same sirvente he says :

Every day I am resoling and sewing up the barons and re-melting them and warming them over, for I thought to get them started (loosen them up), but I am indeed a fool to bother with the business, for they are of worse workmanship than the iron (statue of) St. Lunart, wherefore a man's an ass who troubles about them.

Every day I contend and contest and skirmish, and defend and carry backward and forward the battle ; and they destroy and burn my land, and make wreck of my trees, and scatter the corn through the straw, and I have no enemy, bold or coward, who does not attack me.

Much of such song is, of course, filled with politics and personal allusions which today require explanation. The passages on the joy of war, however, enter the realm of the universal, and can stand without annotation.

" Quan vey pels vergiers desplegar."

When I see the standards spread through the gardens
Yellow and indigo and blue,
The cries of the horses are sweet to me,
And the noise of jongleurs from tent to bivouac,
The trumpets and horns and shrill clarions.
Wherefore I would make me a sirvente,
Such as the Count Richard shall hear it.

And it follows, with every man called by his own name. Another begins :

The Count[7] has commanded and moved me by Sir Arramon Luc d'Esparro, to make such a chanson as shall cut a thousand shields, and wherein (or whereby) shall be broken and shattered helms and hauberks and hoquetons[8] and pourpoints[9].

[6]*Maille*—little round discs.
[7] Ramon V, Count of Toulouse (1148-94).
[8] *Hoquetons*—mail jackets.
[9] *Pourpoints*—the steel collars worn below the helmets.

Besides the political songs and the lament for Prince Henry Plantagenet, " Si tuit li dol elh plor elh marimen," above mentioned, and one beginning, " My songs have end in anguish and in dole." Bertrans has left a number of love songs, among which is the unique *Dompna Soisseubuda* ("The Borrowed Lady ").

Maent of Montagnac has turned him out, and he for consolation seeks to make a " borrowed " or ideal lady ; to which end he, in this song, begs from each pre-eminent lady of Provence, some gift, or some quality : of Anhes, her hair golden as Ysolt's ; of Cembelins, the expression of her eyes ; of Aelis, her easy speech ; of the Viscountess of Chales, her throat and her two hands ; of Bels-Miralhs (Fair-Mirror), her gaiety.

Bertrans finds the song small consolation, as the patchwork mistress does not reach the lofty excellence of Maent. De Born is at his best in the war songs :

Well pleaseth me the sweet time of Easter
That maketh the leaf and the flower come out.
And it pleaseth me when I hear the clamor
Of the birds, their song through the wood ;
And it pleaseth me when I see through the meadows
The tents and pavilions set up, and great joy have I
When I see o'er the campagna knights armed and horses arrayed.

And it pleaseth me when the scouts set in flight the folk with their
     goods ;
And it pleaseth me when I see coming together after
     them an host of armed men.
And it pleaseth me to the heart when I see strong
     castles beseiged,
And barriers broken and riven, and I see the host on
     the shore all about shut in with ditches,
And closed in with lisses of strong piles.

Thus that lord pleaseth me when he is first to attack, fearless, on his armed charger ; and thus he emboldens his folk with valiant vassalage, and then when stour is mingled, each wight should be yare,

47

and follow him exulting ; for no man is worth a damn till he has taken and given many a blow.

We shall see battle axes and swords, a-battering colored haumes and a-hacking through shields at entering melee ; and many vassals smiting together, whence there run free the horses of the dead and wrecked. And when each man of prowess shall be come into the fray he thinks no more of (merely) breaking heads and arms, for a dead man is worth more than one taken alive.

I tell you that I find no such savor in eating butter and sleeping, as when I hear cried " On them ! " and from both sides hear horses neighing through their head-guards, and hear shouted " To aid ! To aid ! " and see the dead with lance truncheons, the pennants still on them, piercing their sides.

Barons ! put in pawn castles, and towns and cities before anyone makes war on us.

Papiol, be glad to go speedily to " Yea and Nay," and tell him there's too much peace about.[10]

The suggestion in the first Envoi, that war can be waged without risk of too great personal loss to the actual participants, shows that the song has purpose as well as purple wording.

Dante says in *De Vulgari Eloquentia* : " I do not find, however, that any Italian has yet written poetry on the subject of arms " ; and in Provence itself the other troubadours may be said to have satirized the lack of courage, rather than to have praised the acts of carnage, as for example, Sordello. Peire Cardinal is extremely lucid on the imbecility of belligerents and the makers of wars.

Dante's third type, Giraut of Bornelh, most popular of the troubadours, cited for his songs on " Righteousness," will seem rather faint after Bertrans. The comparison would be almost cruel if Giraut had not been so over-praised. Despite his reputation, he has left scarcely one of the finest songs of Provence. Ventadour left us the lark song cited above ; Peire Bremon the Song from Syria ; and Peire Vidal the Song of Breath :

[10] This kind of thing was much more impressive before 1914 than it has been since 1920. The pagentry can still be found in the paintings of Simone Martini and of Paolo Uccello.

Ab l'alen tir vas me l'aire
Qu'eu sen venir de Provensa
Tot quant es de lai m'agensa
Si que quan n'aug ben retraire
Eu m'o escut en rizen
E'n deman per un mot cen
Tan m'es bels quan n'aug ben dire.

Breathing I draw the air to me
Which I feel coming from Provença,
All that is thence so pleasureth me
That whenever I hear good speech of it
I listen laughing and straightway
Demand for each word an hundred
So fair to me is the hearing.

No man hath known such sweet repair
'Twixt Rhone and the Vensa.
Or from the shut sea to Durensa,
Nor any place with such joys
As there are among the French folk where
I left my heart a-laughing in her care,
Who turns the veriest sullen unto laughter.

No man can pass a day in boredom who has remembrance of her, in whom joy is born and begun. He who would speak her praise to the full, has no need of skill and lying. One might speak the best, and yet she were still above the speech.

If I have skill in speech or deed hers is the thanks for it, for she has given me proficiency and the understanding whereby I am a gay singer, and every pleasing thing that I do is because of her fair self, and I have all needful joy of her fair body, even when I with good heart desire it.

Piere d'Auvergne has left us the noted song to the nightingale, which begins : "Rossinhol al seu repaire," "Nightingale, go see my Lady within her bower, and speak with her of my state." Bertrans of Born has left us "The Borrowed Lady," and many singers who gained less fame than Bornelh, seem to have excelled him one by one at all points. Bornelh is facile, diffuse, without distinction of style, without personality. He writes for whomso runs, and he is singable.

49

Coleridge says, with truth : " Our genuine admiration of a great poet is for a continuous undercurrent of feeling ; it is everywhere present, but seldom anywhere a separate excitement."

Another test of the poetic art is the single line. In neither the " undercurrent " nor the single line does Giraut excel the best of his contemporaries.

Yeats gives me to understand that there comes a time in the career of a great poet when he ceases to take pleasure in riming " mountain " with " fountain " and " beauty " with " duty." Giraut of Bornelh seldom reached the point where he ceased to take pleasure in the corresponding banalities. But one must not go too far to the other extreme in estimating him ; allowance is to be made for the hostility of our time toward anything savoring of the didactic in verse ; and long-windedness was no such crime in the Twelfth or Thirteenth Century as it is today. Dante mentions Bornelh four times in the *De Vulgari Eloquentia*, even though this might be discounted by the possibility that Dante was choosing well-known songs for purposes of illustration, and that in the first case the point illustrated by one of Giraut's lines is merely philological.

The second illustration[11] is :

> Per solatz reveillar que s'es trop endormitz

> To awake solace
> Because it has been too long asleep
> And to gather and bring back
> Worth which is exhausted
> I thought to trouble myself," etc.

The third :

> Ara auziretz encabalitz cantars.
> Now you will hear marvellous songs.

[11] *De Vulgari Eloquentia*, II, 2. The third, II, 5 ; the fourth, II, 6.

The fourth :

> Si per mon Sobre-Totz no fos.
> Now if it were not for my Sobre-Totz[12]
>
> Who tells me to sing and be gay,
> Neither the soft season when the grass is born,
> Nor meadows, nor boughs, nor woods, nor flowers
> Nor harsh lords, and vain loves,
> Would be able to put me in motion," etc.

In his best known alba all the verses, except the last, are supposed to be spoken by the friend who is guarding the lovers from surprise, a role which would have fitted Giraut most admirably.

> King Glorious, true light and clarity,
> God powerful, Lord if it pleaseth Thee
> To my companion be thou faithful aid,
> Him have I seen not since the night came on,
> And straightway comes the dawn.
>
> Fair companion, sleepest or art awakened ?
> Sleep no more, arise softly,
> For in the East I see that star increasing,
> That leadeth in the day ; well have I known it
> And straightway comes the dawn.
>
> Fair companion, a-singing I call you,
> Sleep no more, for I hear that bird a-singing
> Who goes crying[13] the day through the wood.
> And I fear lest the " jealous " assail you,
> And straightway comes the dawn.

[12] *Sobre-Totz*—Above All.
[13] *Queren.* The misinterpretation of this word seems to be one of the sacred traditions of Provençal scholarship. The form is probably not from the Latin *quaero*, but from *quaeror*, a deponent with all four participles, habitually used of birds singing or complaining (see Horace : *Carmina Sacra*, 43 ; Ovid, *Amores*, i, 29).

Fair companion, come out to the window,
And look at the signs of the sky ;
Know if I am a faithful messenger.
If you do not do this it'll be to your harm,
And straightway comes the dawn.

" Bel Companho," since I left you
I have not slept nor moved from my knees ;
But I have prayed to God, the son of St. Mary,
That he give you back to me for loyal friendship,
And straightway comes the dawn !

" Bel Companho," out there by the stone porches,
You warned me not to be sleepy.
Since then I have watched all night through until the day.
And now neither my song pleases you, nor does my company.
And straightway comes the dawn !

(Then the lover from inside) :

Fair, sweet companion, I am in such rich delight
That I wish there should come never dawn nor day
For the noblest that was ever born of mother
I hold and embrace, so that I scarcely heed
The jealous fool or the dawn.

One would also note Bornelh's *Flor de Lis* :

Er'ai gran joi qu'ieu 'm remembra l'amor,

Now have I great joy when I remember me the love
That holdeth my heart safe in her fidelity.

Erst came I into a garden full of mingled bird songs. And when I
stood within that fair garden, there appeared unto me the fair Fleur-
de-lys, and took my eyes and seized my heart, so that since then I
have not had remembrance or perception of anything, except her on
whom my thoughts are bent.

She is that one because of whom I sing and weep, etc.

He often makes pleasant lines about the Spring, and pleasant sounds, but so did Guillaume de Poitiers, and Marcabrun, and Giraudon the Red before him, and two hundred more of his contemporaries and followers.

In accounting for the celebrity of this " fellow from Limousin," who uses many words which add nothing to his poems, and whose little to say is eked out long with melody, one must remember that the troubadour poetry was, for the most part, made to sing ; the words are but half the art ; and Giraut may easily have been skilled above all others in devising his airs and tunes ; so that the very faults which estrange the careful reader today may have contributed not a little to the " accord " of word and music, where the subtler effects of an Arnaut Daniel, or an Aimeric de Bellinoi might not have " come over the footlights " when sung. However little claim Giraut may have to a place in world literature, his prominence in his own day may not have been without sound reason.

Three other troubadours are cited by Dante,[14] Aimeric of Bellinoi, delightfully :

> Nuls hom non pot cumplir addreicamen

> No man can so utterly fulfil that which he hath
>   in his heart
> But that so soon as it is spoken out or done, it
>   seemeth a little thing.
> Nor doth one love with a true heart
> After he thinks he loves too securely (or completely) ;
> One so thinking decreases where another advances,
> I never love with such semblance,
> But swear, for her whom I hold most dear in my heart
> That some one loves her more
> And that I think I love her but little.

As I have not come upon the rest of the stanzas which should presumably, follow, I give instead one of his crusading songs :

[14] *De Vulgari Eloquentia*, II, 6.

53

I

Sadly being parted from my love,
I sing with mingled joy and weeping,
For grief and tears and piteousness[15]
Come to me from the Count my Lord
Who hath taken the Cross to serve God,
And I have joy because God
Forwards him, and I wish that Christendom might
Turn through him to rejoicing,
And that the Lord God be pleased and praised.
And since God through his great sweetness[16]
Deputes such a champion, he is
Recreant and craven
Who lags behind, and he is cut off from honor,
And who goes is graced and honored.
Let the going be hope of good, of joy and of grace,
    and of valor and honor, and of deliverance from evil.

V

Much should they be sans fear,
Secure and good warriors,
Those who go, for they will
Have on their side
Saint George, and God will be with them
Who has absolved and commanded them,
And he who dies without doubt (fearing, hesitation)
Will be in heaven crowned martyr,
Yea, that Lord who is called
God and King and Man
Will be his surety for it.

The *razo* on Aimeric of Pegulhan (whom Dante cites after Bellinoi) begins :

This Pegulhan " was of Tolosa, son of a burgher, who was a merchant who had cloth to sell, and he learned canzos and sirventes, but sang very badly, and enamored himself of a ' burgesa ' his neighbor, and this love taught him how to make

---

[15] *Pietà*—meaning also " piety."
[16] *Doussor.*

poetry, and he made her many good canzos. But the husband mixed himself (*se mesclat*) up with him and did him dishonor, and Aimeric avenged himself and struck him with a sword through the head. Wherefore it was convenient (*convic*) for him (Aimeric) to leave Toulouse."

The artless *razo*, with its apparent lack of cohesion, often gives a great deal of information in very few words.

Perhaps that on Daude de Pradas, Canon of Magalona, who knew full well the nature of birds of prey, may be taken as a model of adequate speech : it summarizes his poetic career : " And he made canzoni because he had a will to make canzoni and not because love moved him to it ; and nobody thought much of him or of his songs either."

Dante cites Aimeric de Pegulhan's

Si com l'arbres que per sobrecargar

As the tree by over-bearing breaks and harmeth
    its fruit and itself,
So have I harmed my fair lady and myself.

It is scarcely remarkable through the next verses, and one almost wonders why Dante chose it until we come to the sixth stanza.

But often my smiles turn to weeping
And I like a fool have joy in my grief
And in my death when I see your face,
And you care not when you see me die,
You abandon me and make me
Like a child which a man makes stop crying
With a marabotin.[17]
And then when it has begun to be happy,
The man snatches and takes away what he has given
    it, and then it weeps and makes grief twice as great
    as before.

Here the simile might well have appealed to the Maestro,

[17] *Marabotin*—a farthing.

who wrote " col quale il fantolin corre alla mamma quando ha paura o quando egli è afflitto," at the meeting with Beatrice in the Paradisal field.[18]

There remains of Dante's list, Folquet of Marseille, of whose opening line, " tan m'abelis l'amoros pensamens," he is perhaps reminiscent in Daniel's speech in Canto 26 in the *Purgatorio*.

I say " perhaps," because several Provençal songs open with the phrase, " Tan m'abelis." Thus Sordello, in a song that runs, " So pleasureth me the season newly come ; So grieveth me the dearth of song and joy."

Folquet's song runs :

> So pleasureth me the amorous thought
> Which has come to beset my true heart
> That no other thought can fare there.
> Nor is any other thought now sweet and pleasant to me.
> For I am hers when the grief of it kills me,
> And true love lightens my martyrdom,
> Promising me joy ; but she gives it to me over-slowly,
> And has held me long with fair seeming.
>
> Well I know that all I do is nothing at all,
> And what more can I do if Love wish to slay me ;
> For wittingly he (Love) has given me such desire
> As will never be conquered, nor conquer Him.
> Thus am I conquered, for the sighs have slain me
> So gently, because I have not aid from her whom I desire.
> Nor do I expect it from any other,
> Nor have I power to wish for another love.

Later in the same song,

> But if you wish me to turn elsewhere,
> Part from you the beauty and the sweet laughter,
> And the gay pleasure, that had sent mad my wit ;
> Since, as I ween, I must part me from you,
> Every day are you more fair and pleasant to me,
> Wherefore I wish ill to the eyes that behold you,
> Because they can never see you to my good,
> But to my ill they see you subtly (or speedily).

[18] *Purgatorio*, V, 21.

The " Lesser Arnaut " of Marvoil, possibly overshadowed in his own day by Daniel, who was of the castle of Ribeyrac, has in our day come deservedly to his share of praise : he has sung long and clearly of the Countess of Beziers, to whom :

> Fair is it to me when the wind " blows down my throat,"[19]
> In April ere May comes in,
> And all the calm night the nightingale sings, and the jay,
> Each bird in his own speech,
> Through the freshness of the morning[20]
> Goes bearing joy rejoicingly
> As he lodges him by his mate.
>
> And since every terrene thing
> Rejoices when the leaf is born,
> I cannot keep silent the memory
> Of a love whence I am happy.
> Through nature and usage it happeneth
> That I lean toward joy,
> There, where I did the sweet folly
> That thus comes back into my heart.
>
> More white than Helen is my " fair-adorned,"
> And than a flower that is born,
> She is full of courtesy,
> And her teeth are white with true words,
> Her heart frank, sans villeiny.
> Fresh is her hue, and her hair brown golden.
> May God save her, who hath given her this seignory,
> For never have I seen a nobler lady.

For the simplicity of adequate speech Arnaut of Marvoil is to be numbered among the best of the courtly " makers."

In the VIth Canto of the *Purgatorio* Virgil says :

But see there a soul set alone and solitary looketh towards us, and will teach us the speediest way. We came to him. O Lombard soul

---

[19] *Alena* here is " inspire " in its primary sense, with the " taste " and " feel " of the wind.

[20] *Frescor del mati.*

. . . O anima Lombarda, how wast thou haughty and disdainful,
and is the movement of thine eyes majestic and slow !

Nought is said to us, but let us go on, only watching, in the guise
of a lion when he crouches. Yet did Virgil draw on towards him,
praying that he would show us the best ascent, and he replied not to the
demand, but questioned us concerning our country and our life.

And my sweet guide began, " Mantua . . ." and the shade, so self-
contained, leapt towards him from the place where it first was, saying,
" O Mantuan, I am Sordello, of thy land," and they embraced each
other.

Then follows one great invective beginning :

> Ahi serva Italia, di dolor ostello
> Nave senza nocchiero in gran tempesta
> Non donna di provincie, ma bordello !

Sordello's right to this lonely and high station above the
" valley of the kings " has at times been questioned ; but the
following *sirvente* justifies at least the adjective " disdegnosa."

Now would I mourn for Sir Blancatz with this sound over-faint,
With a sad heart and a wounded, and I have good reason to,
For in him had I both
My Lord and my good friend.
And every valiant good is lost in his death,

And so mortal is the harm (to the virtues)
That I have no suspicion that it will ever be undone, except in this
    wise, that they take his heart out, and have it eaten by the Barons
    who live un-hearted, then they would have hearts worth some-
    thing.

First let eat of the heart—for he hath great need of it—
The Emperor of Rome, if he would conquer
The Milanese by force, for they (now) hold him conquered,
And he lives disherited in spite of his Germans,
And secondly, let the French king eat of it,
Then will he recover Castile that he lost by folly.
But *he* will never eat it if his mother does not wish him to.
For it is easily seen, to his credit, that he never does anything that
    troubles her.

As to the English king, since he is little courageous,
It pleaseth me that he eat well of the heart,
Then will he be valiant and worth something,
And will recover the land because of which he lives starved of all
    worth ;
Since the King of France, knowing his nothingness, took it from him.
Let the Castilian king eat for two, for he holds two kingdoms, and
    isn't good enough for one,
But if he eats, I wager he does it in secret,
For if his mother knew of it, she would beat him with a stick.

I would that the King of Aragon eat of the heart straightway,
For it would make him unload from himself the shame
That he gat this side of Marseille and Amilau, for in no other way
    may he get honor by anything he could say or do.
And afterward I would that they give some (of the heart) to the
    King of Navarre ;
For I have heard that he was of more account as count than (now)
    as king.
And it is wrong when God exalts a man into great power
That lack of pluck make him decline in worth.

The Count of Toulouse hath need indeed to eat of it,
If he remember what (land) he was wont to hold, and what he holds.
For with another heart his loss (lost lands) will not come back,
And it does not look as if they would return, with the one he has
    in himself.
Also the Provençal count has need to eat of it if he remember,
That a man disherited lives hardly, and is worth naught.
And even if he would defend his head effectually
He has need to eat of the heart for the great burden which he bears.

The barons wish me ill for that which I speak well,
But they may know that I prize them as little as they me.
"Bel Restaur," if I may but find grace with you,
Set everyone to my loss (harm) who holdeth me not as friend.

The devotional poetry has attained quaintness via the course
of time. Simplicity it had to begin with.

Guilhem d'Autpol's Alba to the Virgin, " Esperanza de totz
ferms esperans," begins :

59

Hope of all that hope truly indeed,
River of pleasure, fountain of true grace,
Chamber of God, garden whence was born all good,
Repose without end, protector of orphan children,
Consolation of the disconsolate faithful,
Fruit of whole joy, security of peace,
Fort without peril, gate of the saving pass,
Joy sans sadness, flower of life without death
Mother of God, lady of the firmament,
Sojourn of friends, true delight without turmoil,
Of Paradise the light and clarity and dawn.

Glorious, so great is the joy that comes to Thee
Because of him who championeth the world and Thee
That man can say no more good in praising Thee
Tho' all the world were set to praising Thee,
For in Thee are all pleasant bounties,
Joys, honors, healings and charities ;
Orchard of love, in thy precious garden
Descended the fruit that destroyeth our death,
Dry twig giving fruit without seed,
Door of heaven, way of salvation,
Of all the faithful, the light, and clarity, and dawn.

(*The Envoi*)

God give life with joy sans bitterness
In Paradise with all his company
To all who shall speak this Alba.

The same spirit is found again, with a plea for the common
speech, in Peire de Corbiac's

Lady, queen of the angels,
Hope of believers,
Since sense commandeth me
I sing of you in the " lenga romana,"
For no man, just or sinner,
Should keep from praising you,
As his wit befits him,
Be it in " roman " or in " lenga latina,"

Lady, rose without thorns,
Fragrant above all flowers,
Dry branch giving fruit,
Land that gives grain without labor,

Star, mother of sunlight the sun,
In the world there is none like you,
Neither far nor near.
Lady, you are the eglantine
That Moses found green
In the midst of the burning flames.

Lady, star of the sea,
More luissant than all others,
The sea and the wind assail us,
Show us the certain way,
For if you wish to bring us to good harbor,
Nor ship nor pilot have fear
Of the tempest which troubles them
Nor of the swelling of the sea.

In contrast, we find the monk of Montaldon.

The other day I was in Paradise,
Therefore am I gay and joyous,
For most pleasant to me
Was God, he whom all things obey,
Earth, sea, vale and mountain;
And he said to me, " Monk, why comest thou,
Why art not at Montaldon,
Where thou hast greater company "

" Monk, it pleaseth me not
That thou should'st be shut in a cloister . . .
But I love rather song and laughter,
The world is better for them
And Montaldon gets a rake-of."

That is to say the income of the monastic house is increased
by its reputation for hospitality or for having a good jongleur
on the premises.

Peire Cardinal's invectives against the corruption of the
church temporal should be read by anyone interested in the

history of the period. There is in Ida Farnell's *Lives of the Troubadours* some notice of another satirist, Guillem Figieira.

The " Tenzon," or song of dispute, is relatively unimportant in Provence. The most favorable idea of this form is to be gained from the " Fresca rosa aulentissima " of the Sicilian, Ciullo d'Alcamo,[21] but this is nearer to the Pastorella than to the Tenzo, which was not so much a dramatic dialogue as an argument about a theory or on such a question as : which man did Lady Maent honor most ; him on whom she smiled, him whose hand she touched, or him whom she tapped with her foot under the table.

The Pastorella has a peculiar interest in so far as it is one of the roots of modern drama. This form of dialogue is never more sprightly than when used by one of earliest singers, Marcabrun, from whom the following :

> The other day beside a hedge
> I found a low-born shepherdess,
> Full of joy and ready wit,
> And she was the daughter of a peasant woman ;
> Cape and petticoat and jacket, vest and shirt of fustian,
> Shoes, and stockings of wool.
>
> I came towards her through the plain,
> " Damsel," said I, " pretty one,
> I grieve for the cold that pierces you."
> " Sir," said the peasant maid,
> " Thank God and my nurse
> I care little if the wind ruffle me,
> For I am happy and sound."
>
> " Damsel," said I, " pleasant one,
> I have turned aside from the road
> To keep you company.
> For such a peasant maid
> Should not, without a suitable companion,

[21] See Rossetti's *Early Italian Poets*.

1932. Opinion modified by Dr. W. P. Shepard's notes on a " Debat." *Modern Philology*, Nov., 1931.

Shepherd so many beasts
In such a lonely place."

"Sir," she said, "whoever I am,
I well know sense from folly,
Your companionship, sir," so said the peasant maid,
"Even if your companionship were set where it should be,
Whoever had it wouldn't have much to boast of."

"Damsel of gentle bearing,
Your father was a gentleman, he who begot you in your mother,
For she was a courteous peasant.
The more I look at you the more you please me,
And I'd take pleasure in making you happy,
If you were only a little human."

"Sir, all my family and my lineage
I see swinging and drawing the sythe and the plow,
Sir," so spake the peasant maid.
"But there are such folk playing at knighthood
As ought to be doing the same
Six days out of the week."

"Damsel," said I, "gentle fairy,
The stars gave you at your birth a marvellous beauty."
                    Etc. . . .

The adventure is finally brought to a successful termination.
There is a series of Pastorellas by Giraut Riquier, "the last
of the troubadours," which is not without interest. The final
poem of the series begins :

To St. Pos of Tomeiras
I came the other day,
All dabbled with the rain,
Into the power of an inn-hostess,
Whom I didn't know,
And I was greatly surprised when the old woman grinned. . . .

It is the forgotten "toza" or damsel of his earlier pastorals,
and the courtly Riquier, finding that she has a grown daughter,
takes up the old game with the second generation, who is, it
seems, as obstinate as her mother.

63

IV

*The patient reader is welcome to gnaw at the following chapter ;
when she can no longer stand it, we offer the postscript on p. 141.*

Dante tells us that the best narrative poetry of the Middle
Ages was written in the " langue d'oil," the dialect of Northern
France. The subjects of these longer poems, germane to all
mediaeval Europe, are catalogued in the Provençal romance
" Flamenca," in a description of how the jongleurs told tales
at a wedding. The original is quite as crude as the following
translation. Octosyllabic is ordinarily used in such narratives.

> Who would to hear divers accounts
> Of kings and marquises and " countes "
> Could hear them full all he would.
> No ear was there in grievous mood,
> For one there told of Priamus,
> Another spoke of Piramus,
> Another counts fair Helen's worth,
> How Paris sought, then led her forth.
> Another told of Aeneas,
> And of Queen Dido's dolorous pass,
> Abandoned in such wretched state.
> One of Lavinia doth relate,
> Whose note on quarrel-bolt did fly
> To him who watched the tower most high.
> One told of Pollonices,
> Of Tideus and Etiocles.
> Another told of Appolloine,
> How that he held Tyre and Sidoine.
> One there told *King Alexander*,
> Another *Hero and Leander*.

And so on—of Catmus, of Jason and the Dragon, of Alcides,
of Phyllis and Demophon, Narcissus, Phito, Orpheus, Philistine,

64

Goliath, Samson and Delilah, Macabeu ; and of " Julius Cæsar,
how he passed the sea quite alone, and did not pray to Nostre
Senor because he knew no fear of water."

> One spoke of that Table Round
> Where came no man, save he were found
> Fit for the King's recognisance,
> Where never failed their valiance.
> And of Don Gavain spoke there one,
> And of the lion his companion,
> And of that knight Lunette freed ;
> To the Breton maid one there gave heed,
> That held Sir Lancelot in prize
> And gave him "no" for all his sighs.
> Another tells of Percival
> Who rode his horse into the hall.
> One telleth *Eric and Enida*,
> And one *Ugonet of Perida*.
> And one recounts how Governail
> Had for Sir Tristram grave travail
> Another of Feniza saith,
> Her nurse caused her to play at death.
> The *Fair Unknown's Tale* one doth yield,
> And one speaks *The Vermilion Shield*.

And further, of Guiflet, Calobrenan, Quec the Seneschal,
Mordred, Ivet ; the Star of Ermeli ; the trick of the old man
of the mountain; how Karles Maines held Germany.

> Of Clodoven and of Pipi[1]
> One doth all the history tell,
> And one of how from glory fell
> Don Lucifer " per son ergoil,"
> And one *Olivier of Verdun*.
> One speaks the verse of Marcabrun,[2]
> One there tells how Daedalus
> Knew well to fly, while Icarus
> Was drowned for his flippancy.
> Etc. . . .

[1] Clodovic and Pipin.
[2] An early troubador.

Here we have some extended notice of what Dante mentions as " gleanings from the Bible, from compilations of exploits of Trojans and Romans, and the exquisite legends of King Arthur." ("Arturi regis ambages pulcerimae, et quam plures aliae historiae ac doctrinae."[3] We must count the Chançons de Geste, represented in the "Flamenca" by the names Charlemagne, Clovic, and Pipin ; and the didactic poetry not noted in the "Flamenca."

The finest of these songs of action is found not among the French but,

> Sotto la protezion del grande scudo
> In che soggiace il leone e soggioga.

in Spain, beneath that " great shield whereon the lion submits and subdues."

Dante is little concerned with Spain and may not have known the contemporary *Poema del Cid*. The langue d'oc, the Provençal, had held long the lordship of all courtly verse. Even the earlier French efforts towards epic-making[4] seem to have interested him little. This also is just, Virgil being his guide, and the French chançons not being in his day sufficiently old to charm by their mere quaintness.

In Italy the songs of deed are not supposed to be indigenous, and after one has fallen back in sheer exhaustion from the later Italian embroiderings on them, one might wish they had never been imported.

Numerous authorities disagree with my preference of the *Cid*, and consider the *Chançon de Roland* the finer poem ; but in its swift narration, its vigor, the humanness of its characters, for its inability to grow old, the Spanish "geste" seems to me to surpass its French predecessor, and to merit first place in our attention.

[3] *De Vulgari Eloquentia*, I, 10.
[4] One must clearly distinguish between the " romance," and the epic or "geste."

The "Poema del Cid"

From the opening, in his dismantled castle at Bivar, where the scene and speech are not unworthy of Greek tragedy, it is the unquenchable spirit of that very glorious bandit, Ruy Diaz, which gives life to the verse and to the apparently crude rhythm.[5] Looking upon the barren perches of the hawks, and the desolation of Bivar, the Cid, sobbing greatly, says : " I thank thee, Lord Father, who art on high, that this thing has come upon me through mine evil enemies ! " (*i.e.* and not through my own misdeeds). It is in this spirit that he accepts all the odds against him. Next we find it in his buoyant greeting to Albarfanez : " Albricias,[6] Albarfanez, for we are thrown out of the land ! "

After the ride from Bivar, Myo Cid comes to his town house, " su posar," in Burgos, but the King's letters have been before him, and everything is closed against him ; even in his own house they are afraid to meet him, when he comes up the narrow cobbled street, and beats at the door with his mailed heel, they send a child out to a balcony or window, and she repeats, parrot-wise, the exact words of the King's writ. This drawing to the life, the variety of actors who are individuals, not figures, gives the *Poema* much of its vitality ; as the Spanish sense of tableau and dramatic setting give it so much of its charm. Crowded street, variegated trappings of the men, the armor and the pennants ; and round about them a great natural theatre, on the Greek pattern : the castle of Burgos on the hills behind, and the sweep of the fields beneath them ; and in the midst the child, lisping high words, and the grave,

[5] As to its " irregular " metre, I can still see Dr. Rennert manicuring his finger nails in seminar, pausing in that operation, looking over his spectacles and in his plaintive falsetto, apropos someone who had attempted to reprint the *Cid* with ten syllables in *every* line : " Naow effa man had sense enough to write a beautiful poem like this is, wudn't yeow think he wudda had sense enough to be able to keount ep to ten on his fingers *ef he'da wanted tew* ? "

[6] *Albricias*—the messenger-cry for largesse, the reward for having brought good news.

bearded Campeador mounted below her, assenting with as fine a simplicity. It takes but a handful of lines in Spanish.

As in the Greek, or, indeed, as in most moving poetry, the simple lines demand from us who read, a completion of the detail, a fulfilment or crystallization of beauty implied.[7] The poet must never infringe upon the painter's function ; the picture must exist around the words ; the words must not attempt too far to play at being brush strokes.

The next set of tableaux is as vivid as it is different.

Martin Antolinez, *el Burgales de pro*, despite the King's orders, brings supplies to Ruy Diaz, going into voluntary exile by this act. He and the Cid then arrange a hoax on two Jews, Raquel and Vidas. The Cid has been exiled on the false charge of malversation of booty taken at a siege ; he and Antolinez now turn this to their advantage, and repair their lack of funds. Two chests, covered with vermilion leather and studded with gold nails, are carefully filled with sand and offered for pawn, on condition that they be not disturbed for a year. Antolinez's manipulation of the brokers, eager enough for gain to treat with a banished man by stealth, is delightful. The author's humor is shown as he talks of their joy at the great weight of the splendid chests, and in Antolinez's further slyness. "Well, Raquel and Vidas, I've done you a good turn. It seems to me my work is worth a pair of breeches." He gets thirty marks of silver as the price of the breeches.

The next tableau is the Cid's farewell to Dona Ximena at San Pedro Cardena, where he leaves money for her keep with the Abbot. There is none of that disregard of the means of life prevalent in certain types of modern novel.

Then begins the series of my Cid's triumphs. Castejon taken by ambush, the booty re-sold to the Moors, and the town abandoned ; Alcocer taken by the stratagem of a feigned retreat. The Cid is shown to be as well supplied with common-

[7] 1932. Very dangerous statement.

sense as is Quixote with romantic ideals. He says to Pedro
Vermuez, concerning the captives, "We will gain nothing by
killing them, they cannot be sold, therefore let them serve us."

Next, King Tamin besieges them : the odds are overwhelm-
ing, but being unable to escape, they determine to fight.
Vermuez, impatient of attack, rushes on alone, and plants the
ensign in the midst of the Moors, where he maintains it until
rescued. Ormsby brings out much of the motion of the passage
describing the charge of the lances : they are fighting 300 to
3000.

> Trezientas lanças son, todas tienen pendones ;
> Senos moros mataron, todos de senos colpes ;
> Ala tornada que fazen otros tantos son.
> Veriedes tantas lanças premer y alçar,
> Tanta adarga foradar y passar,
> Tanta loriga falssa desmanchar
> Tantos pendones blancos salir en sangre
> Tantos buenos cavallos sin sos duenos andar.

Roughly :

> Three hundred lances are they, with pennants every one ;
> Each man kills his Moor, with single blows 'tis done,
> And now at their returning as many more go down,
> And ye might well have seen there so many lances press and rise,
> And many an oval shield there riven lies.
> The ill-forged coats-of-mail in sunder fly,
> In blood there issue the many bannerets white,
> And many a good horse runs there whom no man rideth. [8]

There is constant drama not only in the action, but in the
contending passions of the actors. When after this victory,
the Cid sends Minaya back to Alfonso with three hundred
caparisoned horses, the King answers :

Three weeks is too little time in which to pardon a man who has

---

[8] Not having Ormsby at hand, I have had to use my own translation, which,
however, follows the assonance of the original.

earned my anger, but since it comes from the Moors, I accept the gift. You, Minaya, I pardon and restore you your lands ; as for the Cid, I say nothing, but anyone who likes, has my permission to join him without fear of having his possessions confiscated.

The Cid moves on to the pine-wood of Tebar, and levies tribute up to Saragossa. Raymond Berengar, Count of Barcelona, spoken of as a Frenchman, is offended and comes against him. Taken unaware, the Cid tries to avoid conflict, is forced into it, boasts of the Galician saddles of his company, wins the battle and the sword " Colada." Berengar is the noble foeman : captive, he refuses to eat for three days, until the Cid promises to free him and two other knights. For his friends' sake he eats and is set free. The Cid wishes him good speed and invites him to come back and have another go at it when he feels inclined. "You can have peace from me, my Cid," replies Berengar, " I've paid enough for one year."

The Valencians have come against him. He says :

Well, we are come into their land, we do them much ill, we levy tribute and drink their wine and eat their bread ; they come to assail us and they are right. Tomorrow we exiles will go out against them and see who deserves his pay.[9]

And in the white of the dawn my Cid went to smite them.

" In the name of the Creator and Sant Iago, smite them, cavalleros with love and great willingness.

For I am Ruy Diaz, my Cid of Bivar ! "

And many a tent-cord you might have seen broken,

And many a pole wrenched up and many a tent lying flat.

After the victory, two Moorish kings are killed ; three years are spent in general operations, driving the Moors back to the sea-coast. Valencia surrenders after ten months' siege, and the " Senna "[10] is set on the Alcazar.

[9] This rhymes with the Quattrocento anecdote of Hawkwood. Passing Monk : " God give you peace, my lord." Capt. Hawkwood : " And God take away your means of getting a living."

[10] *Senna*—banner.

The King of Seville, with thirty thousand men, comes against them and is defeated. The Cid's beard increases in length; he swears it shall be famous among Moors and Christians alike. This is presumably a memory of Charlemagne, " à la barbe chenue."

The warrior bishop Jeronimo appears and is given the spiritual rule in Valencia. He recalls Turpin of the *Chançon de Roland*; but he is a type of the time, and not necessarily a figure borrowed from the older poem.

The Cid sends back to Castile for his wife, and sends a hundred horses to Alfonso.

Here ends the pure " geste " of the Cid, and here or hereabouts, begins the "Romance" of the Cid or rather the "Romance of the Infantes of Carrion."

To Minaya at court come Raquel and Vidas demanding repayment. They are put off. In court appear Garcia Ordonez, grumbling about my Cid, and the Infantes of Carrion whispering together. At Valencia my Cid rides to meet his family, and the newly-taken charger Bavieca is seen for the first time in the poem and is approved for his speed. The Cid takes his wife and daughters to the Alcazar to show them his captured city and the sea.

Next March, Morocco comes against them with fifty thousand men; " 4000 less 30 has my Cid." After the victory the tent of the King of Morocco is sent to Alfonso. Garcia Ordonez grumbles. The Infantes openly ask the Cid's daughters from Alfonso. The King offers pardon to my Cid and suggests the marriages. The King is spoken of as " Alfonso, *el de Leon* " (He of Leon). The poem is distinctly Castilian. A meeting is arranged, and the King receives Myo Cid. The Cid says his daughters are too young to marry, but that the King may do as he likes. The responsibility is thus thrown upon the King. The wedding takes place, and the first " Cantar " ends with all living happily in Valencia.

The coplas of this "Cantar" go finishing themselves here.
May the Creator avail you and all the Saints.

The second "Cantar" opens as stageably, if not so seriously, as the first.

The Cid is asleep; his pet lion escapes and terrifies the two Infantes. Ferran takes refuge under the Cid's bed, and Diego, rushing through the door, leaps upon the beam of a wine-press, evidently in use, to judge by his subsequent appearance. My Cid wakes, leads the lion back to his cage, and calls the Infantes, who appear, to the great amusement of the company. My Cid orders silence, but the Infantes consider themselves insulted. Things being in this condition, Bucar comes against Valencia with fifty thousand tents. The Infantes show the white feather, but enter the battle, after which everyone else is described by name as having done valiant deeds. After this the Cid, with irritating magnanimity, still pretends to believe in their valor. The Infantes ask leave to depart with their wives, which is granted.

They plot the death of Avengalon, a Moorish ally of the Cid, who is acting as their escort; but they are detected, and he leaves them alone. They abandon the Cid's daughters in the wood of Colpes, thinking they have beaten them to death. Feliz Munoz, the Cid's nephew, finds the daughters, and the King's vengeance is demanded.

The subsequent scene is arranged in the best theatrical crescendo. In the "Cortes" the third which Alfonso has held, my Cid demands first the swords "Colada" and "Tizon," which he has given to the Infantes; they are granted him. Then his possessions; they also are granted. Then vengeance for the outrage upon his children in the wood of Colpes. Judgment is given. The Kings of Navarre and Aragon appear. The Infantes are killed in combat. The Cid's daughters marry Navarre and Aragon in splendor, and the poem of the Cid ends:

Today the Kings of Spain are of his blood,
To all doth honor increase through him, born in a good hour.
He passed from this life on the day of Cinquessima,
May he have pardon of Christ !
Thus may we all, just and sinners !
These are the tales of my Cid Campeador,
In this place is the telling completed.
May he who wrote this book see God's Paradise, Amen !
Per Abbat wrote it in the month of May, 1245 [11] and in romance.
It is read, give us wine if you have no money.

Upon learning from historical sources that the actual Ruy Diaz of Bivar was not a drivelling sentimentalist, but a practical fighting man, some people speak of disillusion, and marvel (in print) that he came to be chosen the national hero of Spain.

On the outer walls of the church of San Juan de los Reyes, in Toledo, there hang to this day huge rows of heavy old iron fetters struck from Christian captives when the town was last re-taken from the Moors. They may explain at least part of his popularity.

The relation of the Cid of the *Poema* to the historical Cid is outside the scope of this treatise ; the matter is admirably presented by Fitzmaurice Kelly in his *Chapters on Spanish Literature*, from which one concludes that if the Campeador had set out with some beautiful ideals, and an earnest desire to become the idol of ballad writers for the next eight centuries, it is unlikely that he would have taken Valencia ; and although his biographer, had the humor of the Twelfth Century been sufficiently delicate, might have produced an abortive sort of Don Quixote, we should still lack the bravest of " cantares."

Some comparison of the *Poema del Cid* with its French predecessor is inevitable.

The French epopée, according to Gaston Paris, takes its source

[11] At least I believe that is Sr. Ramon Menendez Pidal's opinion as to the reading of the date. Per Abbat is by many supposed to have been the copyist, not the author.

under Clodovic, and becomes apparent in the time of Karl Martel : the three figures, Martel, Charlemagne, and Charles the Bald, are later amalgamated into one heroic figure, " à la barbe chénue."

The *Chançon de Roland*, dating in its present form from the second half of the Eleventh Century, is based upon the historic fact, which an earlier Latin chronicler dismisses thus : " In this battle Edghardus, master of the royal table, Anselmus, count palatine, and Rollandus, præfect of the borders of Brittany, with very many others, were killed." That is, Hrodland, Count of the March of Britanny, commanding the rearguard of Charlemagne's army, was defeated by the Basques in the Valley of Roncevaux, August 15, 778 (A.D.), Charles the Great being at this time thirty-six years of age.

Three centuries later this has solidified into 4002 verses, in what Paris terms the " national style," which style is likely to seem a rather wooden convention to an outlander. The personality of the author is said to be " suppressed," although it might be more exact to say that it has been worn away by continuous oral transmission. Summarizing further, from Paris' lecture on the " *Chançon de Roland* et la Nationalité française " : " You will remember that from their conversion the French proclaimed themselves the people beloved of Christ, chosen by him to defend his church."

This ideal pertains in the *Chançon* ; the enemies are no longer idolaters. They are Mahometans, but the French Christians are little concerned with trifling distinctions, so far as the dramatic proportion is concerned they are " pagans." These pagans held Spain ; the duty of France is to take it away from them, because they have a false religion. The poet's idea is that " The pagans are wrong, the French are right."

When Charlemagne has taken Saragossa, he converts the population *en bloc*.

> En la citet n'est remis paiens
> Ne seit ocis, on devien crestiens.

> In the city remained no pagan
> Who was not killed, or turned Christian.

Paris notes this feeling of national destiny, the love of la douce France, and the love of the national honor, as the three qualities which give the poem its " grandiose character." But we, who have not had our literary interest in the poem stimulated of late by the Franco-Prussian war and the feelings of outraged patriotism attendant thereupon, notice a certain tedious redundance before being charmed by this " caractère grandiose."[12]

The poem is nevertheless quite interesting as a monument to " la nationalité française." Its championship of Christianity against Paganism makes it almost as much of Christendom as of France ; it is most certainly heroic in outline, far more so than the *Cid*.

Threatened by the Franks, the Spanish king and the Sarrasin, Marsille, in Saragossa sues for peace. Ganelon, Charlemagne's ambassador, bears the reply : but, jealous of Roland, he arranges to betray him for a price. Charlemagne, told that Marsille accepts his terms, is, in spite of warning dreams, persuaded to leave Roland behind with the rearguard.

Marsille attacks this rearguard ; Oliver sensibly advises Roland to sound his horn to call back the Emperor. Roland bombastically refuses. The warrior Bishop Turpin blesses the French, but neither Roland's hardihood nor the sanctity of the Bishop avert the natural result. Roland dying, sounds the " olifan," and recalls the Emperor, who is already thirty leagues off. All the rearguard are slain. Charles takes vengeance, aided by Ogier, Geoffrey of Anjou, and the Duke Nayme. Saragossa is garrisoned, and the dead of Roncivaux are buried with honor.

Aude appears for the first and last time, faints, and dies of grief at hearing of the death of her betrothed Roland ; Ganelon

[12] 1932 : I leave what I wrote in 1910. The recent war has not affected this literary equation.

is punished ; the widow of Marsille is converted. " St. Gabriel, de la part de Dieu," tells Charles to start a new war ; and Charles weeps in his white beard at the prospect of carrying a crusade into Syria.

" Ah, la vaillante épopée, chevaleresque et bien française ! " exclaims Leo Claretie. It is, indeed, somewhat French, and Roland is not unlike Galiffet at Strasbourg. We hear somewhat his echo in Cyrano's " quel geste ! " Take this, perhaps the finest passage in the poem, to witness :

> Then Roland felt that death approached,
> His brains rush out through his ears.
> He prays God to receive his peers.
> He confides himself to the angel Gabriel.
> He takes the olifan,[13] to be without reproach,
> And his sword Durendal in the other hand.
> Further than an arblast sends a quarrel bolt
> He goes toward Spain, he enters a field and mounts a hillock,
> Four marble rocks surround two beautiful trees,
> On the green grass he falls backward.
> He swoons, for death is near to him.
> High are the mountains and very high are the trees.
> There are four shining rocks of marble.
> Upon the green grass the Count Roland swoons.
> A Sarrasin had his eyes open,
> Feigning death he lies among the others.
> Blood reddens his body and his visage,
> He rises to his feet and runs forward.
> He was great, of very great bravery.
> Full of pride and of mortal rage,
> He seized Roland, his body and his armor,
> And spoke thus : " The nephew of Charles, conquered !
> This sword will I carry away into Arabie."

Roland awakes, feeling that someone is pulling his sword away from him ; he opens his eyes and says :

[13] *Olifan*—Roland's horn.

"By my faith ! you are not one of us."
He holds the olifan, whereof he would not leave hold.
He smites (the Sarrasin) on the " cimier " all overworked with
    gold,
Despite the steel and the cap within the helmet, and the bones.
The Sarrasin's eyes burst from his head,
He falls dead at his feet
Then he said to him, " Gredin, how were you so hardy,
As to touch me either right or wrong ?
Whoever might hear of it would hold you for a fool.
I have split my olifan,
I have spoiled the carbuncles and the gold."[14]
Then Roland felt that the life went from him.
He rises to his feet as well as he could manage·it,
The color is gone from his visage,
Before him was a brown rock ;
Ten blows he struck in grief and rage,
The steel cracked, but neither broke nor split,
And said the Count, " Saint Mary, aid !
Ah, good Durendal, what dolor !
I can no longer use you, but I do not neglect you !
In how many battles have I conquered with you !
And for such great lands have I battled
To give them to Charles who has the white beard,
You could never belong to a poltroon,
A bold soldier would have kept you long.
Never will there be his equal in free France."
Roland struck upon the rock of " Sardonie."
The steel cracked, but it broke not, nor split.
When he saw that he could not break it
He commenced to lament to himself,
" O Durendal, how white you are,
To the gay sunshine you gleam, you flame ! "

He recalls his past glories, and again tries to break the sword ;
he shivers the hilt, but the blade rebounds and points heaven-
wards ; he prays to the sword in vain, and death comes upon
him.

[14] Landor and his violets !

> There he is lying under a pine ! the Count Roland !
> He wished to turn toward Spain,
> He stretches to God the glove of his right hand :
> St Gabriel received it.
> Then his head falls on his arm,
> He is gone, hands joined, to his end.
> God sent to him His angel Cherubim,
> St Raphael, and St. Michael of Paul.
> St Gabriel is come with them,
> They take the soul of the count to Paradise.

A victim, not to the treachery of Ganelon, but to that pride which forbade him to sound the horn for aid, he dies. Perfect chivalric pose, perfect piety ! The hero goes out of this chançon of gesture, and one feels that perhaps he and the rest of the characters are not wooden figures, that they are simply " latin." Heroic, his hands joined, in death he forgets not etiquette. He is the perfect hero of pre-realist literature.

But as one is grateful for Cervantes after Montemayor, one is grateful for the refreshment of the Spanish *Poema*, and for the bandit Ruy Diaz. I perhaps profane the *Roland* : the death scene is poignant ; parts of it are natural ; all of it might seem natural to minds differently poised. Poetry it has in plenty ; its stiffness may often become, or seem to become, dignity ; but the quality of eternal youth is not in it in such a degree as in the Spanish *Poema*, or in the old captive's song fable, *Aucassin and Nicolette*.

Whatever the *Cid* owes to the *Roland*, it is an immeasurable advance in simplicity ; it is free from such formalizations as in the two trees and four white stones of marble. Indeed, the *Roland* is either too marvellous to be natural or too historical to allure by its mystery. In the realm of magic, the land of the " romances," one expects and demands, haunted fountains, bewitched castles, ships that move unguided to their appropriate havens ; the Breton cycle, the cycle of Arthur, was already furnishing these attractions to the mediaeval audience and supplanting the semi-verities of the " Matter of France."

The third matter, that of " Rome le Grant," need hardly concern us ; it is interesting chiefly in so far as it shows us how vague were mediaeval ideas of antiquity. The *Roland* is the summit of the French cycle ; which is, except for this poem, interesting only now and again, as in the Provençal Geste of *Giraut of Roussillon*, more direct in its style than the *Roland*, or in such incidents as that of the first merry-go-round in the *Pélérinage de Charlemagne*.

The mediaeval critic, fond of trite formulae, and divisions by three, says that the only fit matters for the narrative poet to write about are : the deeds of France, of Britain, and of Rome the Great.

Whatever we can learn from the mediaeval redaction of the events of Greek and Roman antiquity can be more easily learned from the illuminations of an early Fifteenth Century book, which has recently been displayed in the National Gallery. It represents Caesar crossing the Rubicon, he and his hosts being arrayed in the smartest fashions of the late Middle Ages.

The literary artists objected to being bound by actual events, and the folk cry out for marvels. There were ladies to be entertained ; ladies, bored somewhat by constant and lengthy descriptions of combats not greatly differing one from another. The songs of more or less historical happenings went out of vogue ; the romances gradually usurped the first place in interest.

Marie de France is perhaps the most readable of the writers of " märchen." Crestien de Troyes is the recognized master ; while the one immortal tale, the *Tristan*, comes down to us in the versions of Thomas and of Béroul.[15]

Marie's " lais " give us the romantic tales in simpler, shorter form. With them we return to Apuleius, the land of Hear-say.

---

[15] Excellent English version by Belloc.

In a preface addressed to someone called " the King," Marie explains her reason and purpose.

Wherefore I began to think of making some good histories, bringing them from Latin into Romance ; but this meseemed hardly worth while, seeing so many others were already set to it, and then I thought me of the lais which I had heard. I did not doubt . . . nay, I well knew . . . that those who first began them and sent them forth, made them for remembrance of adventures they had heard. Many of them I heard told, and I would not have them forgotten. I have rimed them, and made ditties of them ; many a time have I kept vigil in doing it. . . .

In honor of you, noble king. I have set to gathering the lais, to make rimes and re-tell them.

As these " lais " have been translated, I shall not quote them at length.

Whereat shall marvel all who love, and have loved, and shall love hereafter.

> Ki aiment e amè avrunt
> U ki puis amerunt apres.

There is something like it at the beginning of the *Amadis and Ydoine*.

> Communalement vous qui aves
> Ame et vous qui ore ames
> Et trestuit cil qui ameront,
> Qui esperance d'amer ont,
> Vous qu'aves oi damours
> Selonc le conte des auctours
> Et en latin et en romans . . .

Marie's lay is of Britain the Less ; of Guigemar, who adventureth all things save love alone, until one day a-hunting he sees a white hind with stag's horns. The arrow which he shoots rebounds and wounds him. The hind speaks, telling him that he can get no cure save of one who shall suffer for love of him, so that it will be a marvel to all lovers. In his distress he comes to the sea-board, and finds a magical ship decked with gold and ivory, which takes him oversea to the watergate of a tower, wherein is one prisoned by a jealous lord, and then the story tells of the love. Etc. . . . .

The second tale tells of a slanderous wife and a foundling hidden in an ash tree. The third, of the mountain, " Côte des deux Amants," in Normandy ; and of how the lover trying to carry his girl to the top of it, in compliance with the conditions set by her father, dies of the strain, and she of grief.

The next is of an imprisoned lady, to whom her lover came in the form of a falcon ; amongst the rest are the lays of the Werewolf " Bisclavret " ; of Eiliduc and the ladies Guildeluëc and Guillodun ; of Lanval and the fairy lady that carried him to Avalon ; of Gungeamor, who like Oisin, goes boar hunting and is met by the lady of the fountain, who leads him into a wonderful country for three seeming days, that are three hundred years ; after which he comes back, unbelieving, tells the tale to a charcoal burner, gives him the boar's head, and is received back into the fairy country.

In the lay of *Tyolet* there is an interesting note as to origins. Marie says :

The clerks of the court wrote out the tales in Latin, and from Latin they were turned into Romance, whence, as our ancestors tell us, the Bretons make many a lai.

This, of course, solves nothing : the fairies are Celtic ; the decorative incident is now biblical, now seemingly Ovidian ; and the tales as they stand are a delight to a certain type of reader. They vary in length and in antiquity ; from pre-Arthurian myths, and " lais " that are really short romances, to idylls like that of *The Nightingale*, which might have been based on an incident of Marie's own time.

The work of Crestien de Troyes has been lately translated by W. W. Newell.[16]

The tales move much more swiftly than the similar tales in Malory's *Morte d'Arthur*. Crestien has an eye for the color of mediaeval pageantry and some fidelity to nature. The tales are today what they were to Dante, " the very beautiful legends of King Arthur." As art, they are certainly no advance on Apuleius', *Cupid and Psyche*. They belong to that vast body of pleasant literature which one should read when one feels younger than twenty. There are few people who can read more than a dozen or so of mediaeval romances, by Crestien or anyone else, without being over-wearied by the continual recurrence of the same or similar incidents, told in a similar manner.

It is undeniable that these tales make a definite and intentional appeal to the senses.

Great art is made to call forth, or create, an ecstasy. The finer the quality of this ecstasy, the finer the art : only secondary art relies on its pleasantness.

The Tristan and Ysolt legend stands apart from the other romances. The original energy and beauty of its motif have survived even later versions, and have drawn to them beautiful words and beautiful minor incidents.

The early texts of Thomas and Béroul are reprinted by the Société des Anciens Textes Français. Bedier's reconstruction of the tale from compared texts is available both in his own French and in H. Belloc's English translation. The tale itself is, I presume, familiar in some form or another to everyone.

Tristan, the child of sorrow, is born after the death of his father, Rivalen, King of Lyonesse. He is kidnapped by merchants ; while he is intent on a game of chess aboard their ship, they sail with him to Ireland. Later he comes to live with his uncle, King Mark of Cornwall. He kills the giant Morholt,

---

[16] A. P. Watt and Sons, Publishers, London.

who comes from Ireland to gather tribute (the tale of the Minotaur is somewhere in the background). He goes to Ireland to seek a bride for King Mark ; a dragon is killed ; Tristan is discovered to be the slayer of Morholt. After difficulties, he sets sail homeward with Ysolt. They drink from the magical cup ; love's hand is upon them, and the intrigue of the tale begins.

From here on the tale has been elaborated by various hands. There is discovery ; exile ; life together in the forest of Marrois. Presumably, in some lost version, their tragic death occurs about this time ; but later interest demands that their adventures be prolonged. They are found with a drawn sword between them : they are pardoned by Mark ; restored ; discovered ; Ysolt, tried by ordeal, is unscathed by the heated iron, because her oath of purity is true in letter, though misleading as to fact. Tristan is banished : his adventures with Ysolt of the White Hands, or the second Ysolt, Ysolt of Britany, are interpolated : another giant slain, he returns to Cornwall disguised as a madman. The incandescent fairy dog Pticru creeps into the tale from some Celtic source. The shining house of crystal and rose is discovered by someone ; and a great artist designs the death scene ; remembering Ovid, when he tells of the ship's sails and the fatal confusion of their colors. The Celtic origin of the tale is almost beyond dispute. But one never knows what legends came into Ireland during that earlier period of her culture, the Fifth Century, when Ireland made manuscripts for Europe.

There is a Celtic hall-mark on one of the earlier intrigues, where Tristan sends messages to Ysolt, by dropping marked chips of wood into a stream which flows through her house. The Celts are supposed to be the only people whose primitive lodges were built over a stream in such a way as to make this possible.

In antithesis to this great tragedy, which owes its beauty to its theme, we find the Picard comedy, *Aucassin and Nicolette*, which

owes its immortal youth purely to the grace of its telling. I use
" tragedy " and " comedy " with their looser meaning : Tristan
and Ysolt are doomed from the beginning ; Fate lays their love
upon them ; Aucassin the débonnaire and the fair Nicolette are
born under lighter stars.

> Sweet the song, the story sweet,
> There is no man hearkens it,
> No man living, neath the sun
> So, outwearied, so foredone,
> Sick and woful, worn and sad,
> But is healèd, but is glad
>   'Tis so sweet.

Andrew Lang was born in order that he might translate it
perfectly, and he has fulfilled his destiny, bringing into his
English all the gay, sunlit charm of the original.

Turning to the other monuments of the century, we find one
immensity which nothing has been able to modernize. I mean
The Romaunt of the Rose, which is as much of its time and of
the three succeeding centuries as *The Odyssey* is of all time.

One sees the " romances " preparing for Chaucer ; a part
of the *Romaunt* comes also through the quill of " le grand
translateur," as the " romances " find their prototype in Apuleius'
Cupid and Psyche. So the *Romaunt of the Rose* has Ovid's *Ars
Amatoria* for father ; yet the resemblance is much tempered by
the allegorical-Christian superstructure ; by visions and symbolical figures ; sometimes like Ovid's *Envy* of the *Metamorphoses*, but usually in closer resemblance to the abstractions
of the subsequent mystery plays.

Guillaume de Loris is the springtime of the poem, and John
Clopinel of Meung its autumn. It was nothing new for there
had been much didactic poetry ; yet no poem had such renown
as came to this long-winded, metrical rumination about all
things under heaven.

It is gone, gone utterly, so far as its readableness is concerned.

Youth attempts it once or twice : the philologist might remain suspended, if the language offered him more ground for controversy. Like Persepolis, and the cities of old, there remains a breath of romance in the name, but the site offers little. It has been a great book, the book of Europe for three centuries ; it is now a hunting ground for the intrepidly curious. It has a most interesting " literary position," if one choose to regard it as an unconscious, or semi-conscious, and abortive attempt to do what Dante did triumphantly in the *Commedia*, that is, to " catch the age in a net." This point of view, however, gives the *Romaunt of the Rose* a somewhat exaggerated importance, as neither Loris nor Clopinel seriously attempted to portray humanity. Loris is a pleasant rhymer and Clopinel a tedious theorist. The poem is, nevertheless, interesting to anyone who is studying the progress of the art of narrative.

Objective narrative art precedes the subjective narrative. We have had short poems of emotion and expressions of personal feeling, we have had the tales, but with the *Romaunt of the Rose* we come to a third thing. (*The Rose* is not the first, but the best example for our purpose). Striving for something to relieve the shallowness of the objective romances, we find the allegory, a sort of extension of the fable. The mediaeval author is not yet able to shed himself in completely self-conscious characters ; to make a mood ; slough it off as a snake does his skin, and then endow it with an individual life of its own. In the romances he has told of actions and speech, and has generalized about the emotions. In the allegory he separates himself, not yet from complete moods, but from simple qualities and passions, and tries to visualize them. Thus : Idleness, Jealousy, Youth, Nobility of Heart, are called into being by a sort of inverted Platonic idealism.

My treatment of these long " prose di romanzi " may seem unsympathetic ; but I feel that their interest is archaeological rather than artistic, and that people who can enjoy them are the exception ; barring, of course, the *Cid*, the *Tristan*, the *Aucassin*

85

and Nicolette, and such other poems, or parts of poems, as are needful to satisfy the lay curiosity concerning the literary manner and atmosphere of the time. The modern vogue for them began with William Morris, and passed the zenith when he wrote *Love is Enough*. A more charitable account of them can be found in W. P. Ker's *Epic and Romance*.

.. Postscript. January, 1932.

The problem rises : how far all this mediaeval narrative was literature of escape. The romances were professedly so. But even the " gestes " ? The vitality of the mediaeval lyric was perhaps due to its focussing attention on what was " present." A mystic like Richard St. Victor was much more intent on being alive at the instant in which he was living and writing, than were the narrators.

V

A divagation from questions of technique

Behind the narratives is a comparatively simple state of
" romanticism," behind the canzos, the " love code."

One or two theories as to its inner significance may in some
way promote an understanding of the period.

The " chivalric love," was, as I understand it, an art, that is
to say, a religion. The writers of " trobar clus " did not seek
obscurity for the sake of obscurity.

An art is vital only so long as it is interpretative, so long, that
is, as it manifests something which the artist perceives at greater
intensity, and more intimately, than his public. If he be the
seeing man among the sightless, they will attend him only so long
as his statements seem, or are proven, true. If he forsake this
honor of interpreting, if he speak for the pleasure of hearing his
own voice, they may listen for a while to the babble and to the
sound of the painted words, but there comes, after a little, a
murmur, a slight stirring, and then that condition which we see
about us, disapproved as the " divorce of art and life."

The interpretive function is the highest honor of the arts,
and because it is so we find that a sort of hyper-scientific precision is the touchstone and assay of the artist's power, of his
honor, his authenticity. Constantly he must distinguish between
the shades and the degrees of the ineffable.

If we apply this test, first, as to the interpretive intention on
the part of the artist, second, as to the exactness of presentation,
we shall find that the *Divina Commedia* is a single elaborated
metaphor of life ; it is an accumulation of fine discriminations

---

[1] This chapter was first published in G. R. S. Mead's *The Quest*, about 1916.

arranged in orderly sequence. It makes no difference *in kind* whether the artist treat of heaven and hell, of paradise upon earth and of the elysian enamelled fields beneath it, or of Love appearing in an ash-grey vision, or of the seemingly slight matter of birds and branches . . . through one and the other of all these, there is to the artist a like honorable opportunity for precision, for that precision through which alone can any of these matters take on their immortality.

" Magna pars mei," says Horace, speaking of his own futurity, " that in me which is greatest shall escape dissolution " : The *accurate* artist seems to leave not only his greater self, but beside it, upon the films of his art, some living print of the circumvolving man, his taste, his temper and his foible—of the things about which he felt it never worth his while to bother other people by speaking, the things he forgot for some major interest ; of these, and of another class of things, things that his audience would have taken for granted ; or thirdly, of things about which he had, for some reason or other, a reticence. We find these not so much in the words—which anyone may read— but in the subtle joints of the craft, in the crannies perceptible only to the craftsman.

Such is the record left us by a man whom Dante found " best verse-wright in the fostering tongue," the *lingua materna*, Provençal Langue d'Oc ; and in that affectionate epithet, *materna*, we have a slight evidence of the regard in which this forgotten speech was held by the Tuscan poets, both for its sound and for its matter.

We find this poetry divided into two schools ; the first school complained about the obscurities of the second—we have them always with us. They claimed, or rather jeered in Provence, remonstrated in Tuscany, wrangle today, and will wrangle tomorrow—and not without some show of reason—that poetry, especially lyric poetry, must be simple ; that you must get the meaning while the man sings it. This school had, and has always, the popular ear. The other school culminated in Dante

Alighieri. There is, of course, ample room for both schools. The ballad-concert ideal is correct, in its own way. A song is a thing to sing. If you approach the canzoni of the second school with this bias you will be disappointed, *not* because their sound or form is not as lyric as that of the canzoni of the first school, but because they are not always intelligible at first hearing. They are good art as the high mass is good art. The first songs are apt to weary you after you know them ; they are especially tiresome if one tries to read them *after* one has read fifty others of more or less the same sort.

The second sort of canzone is a ritual. It must be conceived and approached as ritual. It has its purpose and its effect. These are different from those of simple song. They are perhaps subtler. They make their revelations to those who are already expert.

Apart from Arnaut's aesthetic merits, his position in the history of poetry, etc., his music, the fineness of his observation and of his perceptive senses, there is a problem of meaning.

The crux of the matter might seem to rest on a very narrow base ; it might seem to be a matter of taste or of opinion, of scarcely more than a personal predilection to ascribe or not to ascribe to one passage in the canzon " Doutz brais e critz," a visionary significance, where, in the third stanza, he speaks of a castle, a dream-castle, or otherwise—as you like—and says of the " lady " :

She made me a shield, extending over me her fair mantle of indigo, so that the slanderers might not see this.

This may be merely a conceit, a light and pleasant phrase ; if we found it in Herrick or Decker, or some minor Elizabethan, we might well consider it so, and pass without further ado. If one consider it as historical, the protection offered the secret might seem inadequate. I have, however, no quarrel with those who care to interpret the passage in either of these more obvious and, to me, less satisfactory ways.

We must, however, take into our account a number of related things ; consider, in following the clue of a visionary interpretation, whether it will throw light upon events and problems other than our own, and weigh the chances in favor of, or against, this interpretation. Allow for climate, consider the restless sensitive temper of our jongleur, and the quality of the minds which appreciated him. Consider what poetry was to become, within less than a century, at the hands of Guinicelli, or of " il nostro Guido " in such a poem as the *ballata*, ending : " Vedrai la sua virtù nel ciel salita,"[2] and consider the whole temper of Dante's verse. In none of these things singly is there any specific *proof*. Consider the history of the time, the Albigensian Crusade, nominally against a sect tinged with Manichean heresy, and remember how Provençal song is never wholly disjunct from pagan rites of May Day. Provence was less disturbed than the rest of Europe by invasion from the North in the darker ages ; if paganism survived anywhere it would have been, unofficially, in the Langue d'Oc. That the spirit was, in Provence, Hellenic is seen readily enough by anyone who will compare the *Greek Anthology* with the work of the troubadours. They have, in some way, lost the names of the gods and remembered the names of lovers. Ovid and *The Eclogues* of Virgil would seem to have been their chief documents.

The question : Did this " close ring," this aristocracy of emotion, evolve, out of its half memories of Hellenistic mysteries, a cult—a cult stricter, or more subtle, than that of the celibate ascetics, a cult for the purgation of the soul by a refinement of, and lordship over, the senses ? Consider in such passages in Arnaut as, " E quel remir contral lums de la lampa," whether a sheer love of beauty and a delight in the perception

[2] In this *ballata*, Guido speaks of seeing issue from his lady's lips a subtle body, from that a subtler body, from that a star, from that a voice, proclaiming the ascent of the virtu. For effect upon the air, upon the soul, etc., the " lady in Tuscan poetry has assumed all the properties of the Alchemist's stone.

of it have not replaced all heavier emotion, whether or no the thing has not become a function of the intellect.[3]

Some mystic or other speaks of the intellect as standing in the same relation to the soul as do the senses to the mind ; and beyond a certain border, surely we come to this place where the ecstasy is not a whirl or a madness of the senses, but a glow arising from the exact nature of the perception. We find a similar thought in Spinoza where he says that " the intellectual love of a thing consists in the understanding of its perfections," and adds " all creatures whatsoever desire this love."

If a certain number of people in Provence developed their own unofficial mysticism, basing it for the most part on their own experience, if the servants of Amor saw visions quite as well as the servants of the Roman ecclesiastical hierarchy, if they were, moreover, troubled with no " dark night of the soul," and the kindred incommodities of ascetic yoga, this may well have caused some scandal and jealousy to the orthodox. If we find a similar mode of thought in both devotions, we find a like similarity in the secular and sacred music. " Alba " was probably sung to " Hallelujah's " melody. Many of the troubadours, in fact nearly all who knew letters or music, had been taught in the monasteries (St. Martial, St. Leonard and the other abbeys of Limoges). Visions and the doctrines of the early Fathers could not have been utterly strange to them. The rise of Mariolatry, its pagan lineage, the romance of it, find modes of expression which verge over-easily into the speech and casuistry of Our Lady of Cyprus, as we may see in Arnaut, as we see so splendidly in Guido's " Una figura della donna miae." And there is the consummation of it all in Dante's glorification

[3] Let me admit at once that a recent lecture by Mr. Mead on Simon Magus has opened my mind to a number of new possibilities. There would seem to be in the legend of Simon Magus and Helen of Tyre a clearer prototype of " chivalric love " than in anything hereinafter discussed. I recognize that all this matter of mine may have to be reconstructed or at least re-oriented about that tradition. Such rearrangement would not, however, enable us to dispense with a discussion of the parallels here collected, nor would it materially affect the manner in which they are treated. (1916.)

of Beatrice. There is the inexplicable address to the lady in the masculine. There is the final evolution of Amor by Guido and Dante, a new and paganish god, neither Erôs nor an angel of the Talmud.

I believe in a sort of permanent basis in humanity, that is to say, I believe that Greek myth arose when someone having passed through delightful psychic experience tried to communicate it to others and found it necessary to screen himself from persecution. Speaking aesthetically, the myths are explications of mood : you may stop there, or you may probe deeper. Certain it is that these myths are only intelligible in a vivid and glittering sense to those people to whom they occur. I know, I mean, one man who understands Persephone and Demeter, and one who understands the Laurel, and another who has, I should say, met Artemis. These things are for them *real*.

Let us consider the body as pure mechanism. Our kinship to the ox we have constantly thrust upon us ; but beneath this is our kinship to the vital universe, to the tree and the living rock, and, because this is less obvious—and possibly more interesting—we forget it.

We have about us the universe of fluid force, and below us the germinal universe of wood alive, of stone alive. Man is— the sensitive physical part of him—a mechanism, for the purpose of our further discussion a mechanism rather like an electric appliance, switches, wires, etc. Chemically speaking, he is *ut credo*, a few buckets of water, tied up in a complicated sort of fig-leaf. As to his consciousness, the consciousness of some seems to rest, or to have its center more properly, in what the Greek psychologists called the *phantastikon*. Their minds are, that is, circumvolved about them like soap-bubbles reflecting sundry patches of the macrocosmos. And with certain others their consciousness is " germinal." Their thoughts are in them as the thought of the tree is in the seed, or in the grass, or the grain, or the blossom. And these minds are the more poetic, and they affect mind about them, and transmute it as the seed the earth. And this latter sort of mind is close on the vital universe ; and the strength of the Greek beauty rests in this, that it is ever at the interpretation of this vital universe, by its signs of gods and godly attendants and oreads.

In the Trecento the Tuscans are busy with their *phantastikon*. In Provence we may find preparation for this, or we may find faint *reliqua* of the other consciousness ; though one misses the pantheon. Line after line of Arnaut will repeat from Sappho, but the whole seems curiously barren if we turn suddenly from the Greek to it.

After the Trecento we get Humanism,[4] and as the art is carried northward we have Chaucer and Shakespeare, (Jacques-père). Man is concerned with man and forgets the whole and the flowing. And we have in sequence, first the age of drama, and then the age of prose. At any rate, when we do get into contemplation of the flowing we find sex, or some correspondance to it, " positive and negative," " North and South," " sun and moon," or whatever terms of whatever cult or science you prefer to substitute.

For the particular parallel I wish to indicate, our handiest illustrations are drawn from physics : 1st, the common electric machine, the glass disc and rotary brushes ; 2nd, the wireless telegraph receiver. In the first we generate a current, or if you like, split up a static condition of things and produce a tension. This is focussed on two brass knobs or " poles." These are first in contact, and after the current is generated we can gradually widen the distance between them, and a spark will leap across it, the wider the stronger, until with the ordinary sized laboratory appliance it will leap over or around a large obstacle or pierce a heavy book cover. In the telegraph we have a charged surface—produced in a cognate manner—attracting to it, or registering movements in the invisible aether.

---

[4] The Italian, not the recent American brand.

Substituting in these equations a more complex mechanism and a possibly subtler form of energy is, or should be, simple enough. I have no dogma, but the figures may serve as an assistance to thought.

It is an ancient hypothesis that the little cosmos " corresponds " to the greater, that man has in him both " sun " and " moon." From this I should say that there are at least two paths—I do not say that they lead to the same place—the one ascetic, the other for want of a better term " chivalric." In the first the monk or whoever he may be, develops, at infinite trouble and expense, the secondary pole within himself, produces his charged surface which registers the beauties, celestial or otherwise, by " contemplation." In the second, which I must say seems more in accord with " mens sana in corpore sano " the charged surface is produced between the predominant natural poles of two human mechanisms.

Sex is, that is to say, of a double function and purpose, reproductive and educational ; or, as we see in the realm of fluid force, one sort of vibration produces at different intensities, heat and light. No scientist would be so stupid as to affirm that heat produced light, and it is into a similar sort of false ratiocination that those writers fall who find the source of illumination, or of religious experience, centred solely in the philo-progenitive instinct.

The problem, in so far as it concerns Provence, is simply this : Did this " chivalric love," this exotic, take on mediumistic properties ? Stimulated by the color or quality of emotion, did that " color " take on forms interpretive of the divine order ? Did it lead to an " exteriorization of the sensibility," and interpretation of the cosmos by feeling ?

For our basis in nature we rest on the indisputable and very scientific fact that there are in the " normal course of things " certain times, a certain sort of moment more than another, when a man feels his immortality upon him. As for the effect of this phenomenon in Provence, before coming to any judgment upon it we should consider carefully the history of the various cults or religions of orgy and of ecstasy, from the simpler Bacchanalia to the more complicated rites of Isis or Dionysus —sudden rise and equally sudden decline. The corruptions of their priesthoods follow, probably, the admission thereto of one neophyte who was not properly " sacerdos."

There are, as we see, only two kinds of religion. There is the Mosaic or Roman or British Empire type, where someone, having to keep a troublesome rabble in order, invents and scares them with a disagreeable bogie, which he calls god.

Christianity and all other forms of ecstatic religion, on the other hand, are not in inception dogma or propaganda of something called the *one truth* or the *universal truth* ; they *seem* little concerned with ethics ; their general object appears to be to stimulate a sort of confidence in the life-force. Their teaching is variously and constantly a sort of working hypothesis acceptable to people of a certain range of temperament—a " regola " which suits a particular constitution of nerves and intellect, and in accord with which the people of this temperament can live at greatest peace with " the order," with man and nature. The old cults were sane in their careful inquisition or novitiate, which served to determine whether the candidates were or were not of such temper and composition.

One must consider that the types which joined these cults survived, in Provence, and survive, today—priests, maenads and the rest—though there is in our society no provision for them.

I have no particular conclusion to impose upon the reader ; for a due consideration of Provençal poetry in " trobar clus," I can only suggest the evidence and lines of inquiry. The Pauline position on wedlock is of importance—I do not mean its general and inimical disapproval, but its more specific utterances. Whatever one may think of the pagan survivals in Mariolatry or of the cult of virginity, it is certain that nothing exists without due cause or causes. The language of the Christian mystics concerning the " bride " and the rest of it ; the ancient ideas of union with the god, or with Queen Isis—all these, as " atmospheric influences," must be weighed ; together with the testimony of the arts, and their progression of content.

In Catullus' superb epithalamium " Collis O Heliconii," we find the affair is strictly on one plane ; the bride is what she is in Morocco today, and the function is " normal " and eugenic. It is the sacrificial concept. Yet Catullus, recording his own emotion, could say : " More as a father than a lover." Propertius writes : " Ingenium nobis ipsa puella fecit."

Christianity had, one might say, brought in the mystic note ; but this would be much too sweeping. Anatole France, in his commentary on Horace's " Tu ne quaesaris," has told us a good deal about the various Oriental cults thronging the Eternal City. At Marseille the Greek settlement was very ancient. How much of the Roman tone, or the Oriental mode, went out from Rome to the Roman country houses which were the last hold of culture, we can hardly say ; and from the end of the Sixth Century until the beginning of the Twelfth there is supposed to be little available evidence. At least we are a fair distance from Catullus when we come to Peire Vidal's : " Good Lady, I think I see God when I gaze on your delicate body."

You may take this if you like *cum grano*. Vidal was confessedly erratic. Still it is an obvious change from the manner of the Roman classics, and it cannot be regarded as a particularly pious or Christian expression. If this state of mind was fostered by the writings of the early Christian Fathers, we must regard their influence as purely indirect and unintentional.

Richard St. Victor has left us one very beautiful passage on the splendors of paradise.

They are ineffable and innumerable and no man having beheld them can fittingly narrate them or even remember them exactly. Nevertheless by naming over all the most beautiful things we know we may draw back upon the mind some vestige of the heavenly splendor.

I suggest that the troubadour, either more indolent or more logical, progresses from correlating all these details for purpose of comparison, and lumps the matter. The Lady contains the catalogue, is more complete. She serves as a sort of *mantram*.

" The lover stands ever in unintermittent imagination of his lady (co-amantis)." This is clause 30 of a chivalric code in Latin, purporting to have been brought to the court of Arthur. This code is not, I should say, the code of the " trobar clus," not the esoteric rule, but such part of it as has been more generally propagated for the pleasure of Eleanor of Poictiers or Marie de Champagne.

Yet there is, in what I have called the " natural course of events," the exalted moment, the vision unsought, or at least the vision gained without machination.

Though the servants of Amor went pale and wept and suffered heat and cold, they came on nothing so apparently morbid as the " dark night." The electric current gives light where it meets resistance. I suggest that the living conditions of Provence gave the necessary restraint, produced the tension sufficient for the results, a tension unattainable under, let us say, the living conditions of imperial Rome.

So far as " morals " go, or at least a moral code in the modern sense, which might interfere in art, Arnaut can no more be accused of having one than can Ovid.[5] Yet the attitude of the Latin *doctor amoris* and that of the *gran maestro de amor* are notably different, as for instance on such a matter as delay. Ovid takes no account of the psychic function.

It is perhaps as far a cry from a belief in higher affection to a mediumistic function or cult of Amor, as is the latter from Ovid. One must consider the temper of the time, and some of the most interesting evidence as to this temper has been gathered by Remy de Gourmont, in *Le Latin Mystique*, from which :

[5] Ovid, outside his poetry, perhaps, superficially had one.

97

> Qui pascis inter lilia
> Septus choreis virginum.
> Quocumque pergis virgines
> Sequntur, atque laudibus
> Post te canentes cursitant,
> Hymnosque dulces personant[6]

> Who feedest 'mid the lilies,
> Ringed with dancing virgins
> Where'er Thou runnest, maidens
> Follow, and with praises
> Run behind Thee singing,
> Carolling their hymns.

Or :

> Nard of Columba flourisheth ;
> The little gardens flame with privet ;
> Stay the glad maid with flowers,
> Encompass her with apple boughs.[7]

As for the personae of the Christian cult they are indeed treated as pagan gods—Apollo with his chorus of Muses, Adonis, the yearly slain, " victima paschalis,"[8] yet in the " sequaire " of Godeschalk, a monk in the Eleventh Century, we see a new refinement, an enrichment, I think, of paganism. The god has at last succeeded in becoming human, and it is not the beauty of the god but the personality which is the goal of the love and the invocation.

The Pharisee murmurs when the woman weeps, conscious of guilt. Sinner, he despises a fellow-in-sin. Thou, unacquainted with sin, hast regard for the penitent, cleansest the soiled one, loved her to make her most fair.

She embraces the feet of the master, washes them with tears, dries

---

[6] From *Hymns to Christ.*

[7] From *Ode on St. Colum.*

[8] There is a magnificent thesis to be written on the role of Fortune, coming down through the Middle Ages, from pagan mythology, via Seneca, into Guido and Dante.

them with her hair ; washing and drying them she anointed them with unguent, covered them with kisses.

These are the feasts which please thee, O Wisdom of the Father ! Born of the Virgin, who disdained not the touch of a sinner.

Chaste virgins, they immaculately offer unto the Lord the sacrifice of their pure bodies, choosing Christ for their deathless bridegroom.

O happy bridals, whereto there are no stains, no heavy dolors of childbirth, no rival mistress to be feared, no nurse molestful !

Their couches, kept for Christ alone, are walled about by angels of the guard, who, with drawn swords, ward off the unclean lest any paramour defile them.

Therein Christ sleepeth with them : happy is this sleep, sweet the rest there, wherein true maid is fondled in the embraces of her heavenly spouse.

Adorned are they with fine linen, and with a robe of purple ; their left hands hold lilies, their right hands roses.

On these the lamb feedeth, and with these is he refreshed ; these flowers are his chosen food.

He leapeth, and boundeth and gamboleth among them.

With them doth he rest through the noon-heat.

It is upon their bosoms that he sleepeth at mid-day, placing his head between their virgin breasts.

Virgin Himself, born of a virgin mother, virginal retreats above all he seeketh and loveth.

Quiet is his sleep upon their bosoms, that no spot by any chance should soil His snowy fleece.

Give ear unto this canticle, most noble company of virgin devotees, that by it our devotion may with greater zeal prepare a temple for the Lord.

With such language in the cloisters, would it be surprising that the rebels from it, the clerks who did not take orders, should have transferred something of the manner, and something of the spirit, to the beauty of life as they found it, that souls who belonged, not in heaven but, by reason of their refinement, somewhat above the mortal turmoil, should have chosen some middle way, something short of grasping at the union with the absolute, nor yet that their cult should have been extra-marital ? Arnaut was taught in cloister, Dante praises certain " prose di romanzi " and no one can say precisely whether or no they were such *prose* for music as the Latin sequence I have just quoted. Yet one would be rash to affirm that the " passada folor " which he laments[9] at almost the summit of the purifying hill, and just below the earthly paradise, was anything more than such deflection.

CHRONOLOGICAL CHART

Scotus Eriugina, died 877		Arab philosophers Alkindi, died 870 Comment on Aristotle Avicenna, born 980
Guillaume de Poitiers 1071–1127		
circa 1190 Bertrans de Born Plantagenets Arnaut Daniel Philippe August	1170 . . . 1228 Vogelweide Hauenstaufen Curious lack of personality in Sicilian poetry. Falcon Book.	Averroes, died 1198 German translations of Ovid & The Song of Songs. Albert von Halberstadt.
Guillaume Figueira Albigeois infamy	Sordello Eccelin Charles of Anjou 1200–1269	Aristotle translated into Latin & forbidden.
	1250 Death of Frederic of Sicily Birth of Guido Cavalcanti	Albertus Magnus 1193–1280 Fat-headed Aquinas 1227–1274 Grosseteste

The period might be made more transparent by a more thorough table of dates; affiliations of troubadours and dynasties; of books available or newly active at a given time.

---

[9] *Purgatorio,* Canto 26.

VI

> *Il mille cento trentacinque nato*
> *Fo questo tempio, a Zorzi consecrato*
> *Fo Nicolau scolptore*
> *E Glielmo fo l'autore.*
> Inscription over the arch of the
> great altar in the Cathedral Church
> of Ferrara.

While Lorris and Clopinel were compiling their encyclopedia of what passed for wisdom, the tradition of Provence was being continued in Tuscany.

The Albigensian Crusade, a sordid robbery cloaking itself in religious pretence, had ended the *gai savoir* in southern France. The art of the troubadours meets with philosophy at Bologna and a new era of lyric poetry is begun.

Perhaps the most notable poem of the transition is the Sicilian Ciullo d'Alcamo's "Fresca rosa aulentissima," to be found translated in D. G. Rossetti's *Early Italian Poets*.

The poetry of St. Francis of Assisi stands somewhat apart from the line of secular development. Some knowledge of this sort of poetry is necessary if one wishes to understand the period or to appreciate fully certain passages in the *Divina Commedia* ; as is also some acquaintance with that vast amount of prose concerning the lives of saints. The most beautiful work of this sort is the *Fioretti* of St. Francis. Of its hero's compositions, the finest is the *Cantico del Sole*, wherein that "little sheep of God" speaks to the glory of the Father Eternal in a free, unrhymed verse with a rhythm strong as the words and well accompanying them :

Most high Lord,
Yours are the praises,
The glory and the honors,
And to you alone must be accorded
All graciousness ; and no man there is
Who is worthy to name you.
Be praisèd, O God, and be exalted,
My Lord, of all creatures,
And in especial of the most high Sun
Which is your creature, O Lord, that makes clear
The day and illumines it,
Whence by its fairness and its splendor
It is become thy face ;
And of the white moon (be praisèd, O Lord)
And of the wandering stars,
Created by you in the heaven
So brilliant and so fair.
Praisèd be my Lord, by the flame
Whereby night groweth illumined
In the midst of its darkness,
For it is resplendent,
Is joyous, fair, eager ; is mighty.
Praisèd be my Lord, of the air,
Of the winds, of the clear sky,
And of the cloudy, praisèd
Of all seasons whereby
Live all these creatures
Of lower order.
Praised be my Lord
By our sister the water,
Element meetest for man,
Humble and chaste in its clearness.
Praisèd be the Lord by our mother
The Earth that sustaineth,
That feeds, that produceth
Multitudinous grasses
And flowers and fruitage.
Praisèd be my Lord, by those
Who grant pardons through his love,
Enduring their travail in patience
And their infirmity with joy of the spirit.
Praisèd be my Lord by death corporal

Whence escapes no one living.
Woe to those that die in mutual transgression
And blessed are they who shall
Find in death's hour thy grace that comes
From obedience to thy holy will,
Wherethrough they shall never see
The pain of the death eternal.
Praise and give grace to my Lord,
Be grateful and serve him
In humbleness e'en as ye owe.
Praise him all creatures !

The text given in Paul Sabatier's *Vie de S. François d'Assise* reads " brother sun," " sister moon and the stars," " brother wind," " brother fire." This, of course, accords with the practice in the *Fioretti* ; but the rhythm in Sabatier's text seems to me much less impassioned than that in the one I have translated, also its greater length is against its being the earlier version.

For myself, " blanca luna " and " vaghe stelle " seem equally poetical ; but personal preference aside, the shorter, simpler form, the more vigorous, ecstatic rhythm, the version conforming less to the mannerisms of the *Fioretti*, seems more probably to be the work of Francis himself. Rhythm is the hardest quality of a man's style to counterfeit, and here one should compare the rhythm of the different versions of the Cantico del Sole to that of other Franciscan poems, remembering that St. Francis' rhythm is always influenced by the drone of the church services.

The first Italian who can be said to have advanced the art of poetry is Guido Guinicelli of Bologna, the " Maximus Guido " of Dante's Latin works. So far as I can discern he was the first writer to discover that a certain form of canzone stanza is complete in itself. This form of stanza, standing alone, we now call the " sonnet." If Guido did not invent this form, he is, at least, the first who brought it to perfection. He also introduced into romance poetry that new style in which the eyes and the heart and the soul have separate voices of their own, and converse together. It is true that he deliberates—overmuch for poetical purposes—on the state of man in this life and the next, but this must be forgiven him, seeing that he opened new paths at a time when imitation of Provence was over-servile.

Provence had had much paganism, unacknowledged, some heresy[1] openly proclaimed, and a good deal of conventional piety. Unquestioning they had worshipped Amor and the more orthodox divinities, God, Christ, and the Virgin. From Amor or his self-constituted deputies they had received a code of laws. To God and his saints they had prayed incuriously.[2]

The Tuscan bookworms suddenly find themselves in the groves of philosophy, God becomes interesting, and speculation, with open eyes and a rather didactic voice, is boon companion to the bard.

Thought, which in Provence had confined itself to the manner, now makes conquest of the matter of verse.

Abandon hope all ye who enter upon any extended study of this period without some smattering of scholastic philosophy. Hell we have had in Pindar and Virgil ; heaven, somewhat, in Plato ; but the Tuscan poets gambol through the complicated Aquinean universe with an inconsequent preciseness which bewilders one accustomed to nothing more complex than modern civilization.

Guinicelli escapes from labyrinthine circumplications in the famed and beautiful canzone which Rossetti has translated :

> Within the gentle heart Love shelters him,
> As birds within the green shade of the grove.
> Before the gentle heart, in Nature's scheme
> Love was not, nor the gentle heart ere Love.

. . . . . .

---

[1] Jos. McCabe's *Life of Abelard* will give a fair idea of what the term heresy might mean in the Middle Ages. It is a most interesting account of this poet, whose love poems have perished. Abelard, as we know him, is the knight-errant of learning. He gave up his inheritance for study, as Daniel left learning to become a jongleur.

[2] That is to say, Scotus Eriugina was probably not very widely read in Limosi.

The fire of Love comes to the gentle heart
Like as its virtue to a precious stone ;
To which no star its influence can impart
Till it is made a pure thing by the sun.

Rossetti has not translated this sonnet beginning :

Vedut' ho la lucente stella diana.

I have seen the shining star of the dawn
Appearing ere the day yieldeth its whiteness.
It has taken upon itself the form of a human face,
Above all else meseems it gives splendor.
A face of snow, color of the ivy-berry,
The eyes are brilliant, gay, and full of love,
And I do not believe that there is a Christian maid in the world
So full of fairness or so valorous.
Yea, I am so assailed of her worth,
With such cruel battling of sighs,
That I am not hardy to return before her ;
Thus may she have cognizance of my desires :
That without speaking, I would be her servitor
For naught save the pity that she might have of my anguish.

Here the preciseness of the description denotes, I think, a
clarity of imaginative vision. In more sophisticated poetry an
epithet would suffice, the picture would be suggested. The
dawn would be "rosy-fingered" or "in russet clad." The
Tuscan poetry is, however, of a time when the seeing of visions
was considered respectable, and the poet takes delight in definite
portrayal of his vision. The use of epithet is an advance on
this method only when it suggests a vision not less clear, and its
danger is obvious. In Milton or Swinburne, for example, it
is too often merely a high-sounding word and not a swift
symbol of vanished beauty. My use of "valorous" is archaic
and perhaps unpardonable, but the orthodox word "worthy"
has no aroma.

Rossetti gives the following sonnet, but it would take several translations and some comment to exhaust the beauty of the original :

Io vo del ver la mia donna lodare.

The octave :

I wish with truth to speak my Lady's praise,
And liken her to rose and gilly flower,
More than the dawn star's grace her splendor is.
The green stream's marge is like her, and the air,
And all her colors are yellow flowers and red.
Gold and silver and rich joys become more rarified,
Yea, Love himself meseems refined through her.

In this connection one must remember that alchemy and mystical philosophy interpenetrate each other, and that feminine names were used as charms or equations in alchemy. Here the word " raffina " recalls a similar line in Arnaut Daniel.

The sestet :

She goes her way adorned so graciously
That pride forsakes whom she graces with greeting.
Yea, he betrays our faith who creeds her not.
No man impure may venture near to her.
Yet would I tell you of a greater worth :
There is no man whose evil thoughts do not cease a little while before
    she appears.

Rossetti renders the last line beautifully : " No man could think base thoughts who looked on her," but " finche la vede " seems to imply that her spiritual influence would reach somewhat beyond her visible presence.

The distinction may seem over-precise, but it is in the spirit of this period to be precise. It is to be remembered also that Rossetti is substituting verse in one language for verse in another, while the translations in this book are merely exegetic.

The following passage from one of Guinicelli's canzoni serves to illustrate how the Tuscan grammatical structure differs from the Provençal. The bracketed words are not in the original.

For Lo ! the star which measures our time
Is like that lady who hath lit my love.
Placed in Love's heaven she is,
And as that other (star) by countenance
From day to day illumineth the world
So doth she (illumine) the hearts
Of gracious folk and all the valorous,
With but the light which rests in her face ;
And each man honors her,
Seeing in her the light all perfectèd
Which bears full virtue to the minds
Of all, who (thereby) grow enamored,
And such is she who colors
The heaven with light, being guide of the true-hearted
With a splendor which lures by its fairness.

The directness of Provençal song has here been lost. The complicated system of introactive relative clauses could only have been set down by a man accustomed not so much to hear poetry as to read it, one would say, in Latin.

The subject matter of these passages from the ode beginning " Avvegna ched eo m' aggio più per tempo," forebodes the " dolce stile " of Dante.

Although long time I had cried out
Un'vailingly for pity and for love
Wherewith to comfort this grievous life of ours
My time's not yet outrun,
Thus, since my speech yet finds not your heart,
I stand a-weeping with my wounded soul,
Saying together : ' Thus was it cast in heaven.'

O blessed joy whereon man calleth ever,
Oimè ! and when and how
Shall come my power to see you visibly ?
So that in this present hour I might make you aid of comfort
Therefore hear me, for my speech pertaineth,
And give rest to my love-wrought sighs.

> Yea, we prove that in this blinded world
> Each one has life of anguish and grief,
> Fortune bedraggling man through all mischance
> Ere he win heaven wherein is perfect joy.

The Fifth Stanza :

> Reflect upon the pleasure, then, where dwelleth
> Your Lady who is crowned in heaven,
> In whom rests your hope of Paradise ;
> (Reflect) with your every holy memory
> Contemplating a soul set in heaven,
> Your heart, which is hereby bewildered,
> Has painted within it this so blessed face,
> Whose semblance below is as the miracle above,
> (Has painted within it) even more, since it is known how she was
> received by the angels ;
> This your spirits have reported, (spirits) who many a time make
> the voyage.[3]

> *Coda* :

> > She speaks of you with the blessed,
> > And says to them : ' while I was in the world
> > I received honor from him,
> > In so much as he praised me in his songs of praise,'
> > And she prays to God, the true Lord,
> > That he comfort you, as shall please you.[4]

This passage shows us two things ; it shows us that certain conceits of Dante's earlier poetry were by no means original ; and it shows us the dangers of the philosophical love song.

You that have changed the manner and the pleasing songs of love, both form and substance, to surpass every other troubadour . . . you surpass every man in subtlety ; but so obscure is your speech, that there is none found to explain it.

[3] I have thought it necessary to insert in brackets the subjects of some of the relative pronouns.

[4] Rossetti attributes this to Cina da Pistoija, and is probably right ; in which case the quotation illustrates only one of my points.

I would further refer you to *The Early Italian Poets* for the translation of " Tegno di folle impresa, allo ver dire,"[5] mentioned by Dante,[6] and for one vivid simile to the sonnet, *Concerning Lucy*.

In Guinicelli we find the root of the " curial style." His contemporaries may for the most part be regarded as a continuation of the Provençal decadence, or as channels wherethrough the Provençal manner was brought into Italy. Following Guinicelli come three men who brought the Italian canzone form to perfection ; they are Guido Cavalcanti (born 1250), Dante Alighieri (born 1265), and Cino da Pistoija (born 1270). With them must be named Fazio degli Uberti, author of the long, didactic, geographical *Dittatiomundi*, and whose glorious ode, " Io miro i crespi e gli biondi capegli," has been at times attributed to Dante, and printed in his *Canzonieri*. Uberti was born half a century later.

Concerning the lesser lights of the period, Rossetti has written sufficiently in the *Early Italian Poets*, noting the keen satire of Rustico di Filippo, Folgore's sonnets on the days and months, the poems of Lappo Gianni, and of other personal friends of Dante ; the scurrilous sonnets of Cecco Angioleri of Siena, chief opponent of the courtly school ; he gives also translations from Jacopo, " The Notary " of Lentino, Guittone, Bonaggiunta, and Guido delle Colonne, all of whom we find mentioned by Dante either in his prose or in the *Commedia*. The progress of the art after Guinicelli can, however, be sufficiently traced through the works of Cavalcanti, Cino, and Dante.

Cino is best seen in his canzone, *Of Consolation : To Dante upon the Death of Beatrice*, and in the lament for Selvaggia, beginning

> The beautiful bright hair
> That shed reflected gold
> O'er the green growths on either side the way.

[5] " I hold him verily of mean emprise."
[6] *De Vulgari Eloquentia*, ii, 5.

Both poems are given in Rossetti.

The haughty and impetuous elder of the trio, Guido Cavalcanti, was Cino's enemy, and was friend, and later, enemy, of Dante.

Dante himself never wrote more poignantly, or with greater intensity than Cavalcanti. The single line is, it is true, an insufficient test of a man's art, but it is a perfect test of his natural vigor, and of his poetic nature.

In all poetry of the emotions I know nothing finer than those lines of Cavalcanti which Rossetti has rendered :

> When with other women I behold my Love—
> Not that the rest were women to mine eyes
> Who only as her shadows seemed to move.

His poignancy is seen in such lines as :

> Not even enough of virtue with me stays
> To understand, ah me !
> The flower of her exceeding purity.

A spirit more imperious and less subtle[7] than Dante, more passionate, less likely to give ear to sophistries ; his literary relation to Dante is not unlike Marlowe's to Shakespear, though such comparisons are always unsafe. No man has written better ballate, and his individuality is unquestionable ; Rossetti has translated the proof of this in the *Ballata, written in Exile at Sarzana*, which begins, in the translation :

> Because I think not ever to return,
> Ballad, to Tuscany,—
> Go therefore thou for me
>   Straight to my lady's face,
>   Who, of her noble grace,
> Shall show thee courtesy.

And more proof is in that sonnet where he says :

> They worship thy face, Lady, at San Michele in Orto
> . . . where it is a refuge and comfort to sinners.

---

[7] 1929 : I retract this expression. The rest of the sentence stands.

And in the canzone to Fortune, where the rhythm turns as
her wheel :

> Io son la donna che volgo la ruota
> Sono colei, che tolgo e dò stato
> Ed è sempre biasmato
> A torto el modo mio da voi mortali.

> I am the woman who turneth the wheel,
> I am who giveth and taketh away.
> And I am blamed alway
> And wrongly, for my deeds, by ye, mankind.

Rossetti ends it (Fortune speaking) :

> Nor say because he fell I did him wrong,
> Yet mine is a vain song,
> For truly ye may find out wisdom when
> King Arthur's resting-place is found of men.

After a few hours with the originals, criticism becomes a vain
thing. One says with Milton, " Questo è lingua di qui si vanta
amore,"[8] and makes an end,

> Chi è questa, che vien ch' ogni uom la mira
> E fa di clarità l'aer tremare ?
> Who is she coming whom all gaze upon,
> Who makes the whole air tremulous with light ?

Cavalcanti's words are applicable to the song of his time :

> E mena seco Amor, siche parlare
> Null' uom ne puote, ma ciascun sospira.
> And leadeth with her Love so no man hath
> Power of speech, but each one sigheth.

It was the great age of the canzone as the age of Shakespear
was the great age of the romantic drama.

Both Dante and Shakespear were men " born in their due
time."

---

[8] " This is the language whereof Love's self makes boast."

In the age of the canzone the poetry of Christendom was made perfect.

The following unimportant sonnet, 33rd in Dante's *Canzonieri*, will perhaps show how that age set a fashion of poetic speech that pertained with scant variance for some centuries.

Io maledico il di . . .

I curse the day wherein I first saw the light of your eyes traitorous. That moment's self is cursed wherein you mounted first the summit of my heart to draw thence out the soul. I curse the amorous file that has polished my fair speeches, and the fair colors that I have found through you, and set in rhyme to bring it to pass that the world shall henceforth for ever honor you.

And I curse my hard mind that is firm to hold what kills me, that is, your fair culpable face wherethrough Love often perjures him, so that each one, who thinks that Fortune turns the wheel, makes mock of Love and me.

The debt of the English Elizabethan poets to the writers of this period has never been carefully computed. It is, I think, greater than is usually supposed. How " Elizabethan," for instance, is this sonnet from Guido Orlandi to Guido Cavalcanti ·

> Whence moveth love and whence hath he his birth,
> What is his proper stead, wherein he dwelleth,
> And is he substance, accident or memory,
> A chance of eyes, or a desire of heart?
> And whence proceeds his madness or his state;
> Is he a flame that goes devouring
> Or does he nourish? I demand you now:
> How, when and of whom maketh he him lord?
> What thing is Love, I ask, hath he a face,
> Hath he a form by self, or others' likeness?
> Is this love life, or is he death in truth?
> He who doth serve him, should so know his nature.
> I ask thee, Guido, this concerning him
> Since thou art called ' accustomed ' at his court?

I have, in some small measure, pointed out Dante's debt to Guinicelli, a debt which he openly proclaimed.

Dante's greater poetry rises above the age, not because it is, line for line, better, or more essentially poetic, than the best of Guinicelli's or of Cavalcanti's verses, but because of the lofty, austere spirit moving behind the verse. That spirit shows itself in the first tangled canzone of the *Convito* ; an ode, I think, which shows all the faults and all the fineness of the time. Obscure it certainly is, at first reading ; but, when the sense and form are once comprehended, its beauty is a beauty that never tires one. Time after time can one return to it, and always one's hunger for the beautiful is satisfied.

The Italian forms are not, as certain writers have stated, a simplification of the Provençal forms. The rhyming has, it is true, been made easier, but the structure of the stanza is usually more complex. This particular canzone conforms to the rules laid down in *De Vulgari Eloquentia*. The single stanza consists of three parts, the second of which must repeat the rhymes of the first ; the third part is free. The lines may be of eleven and of seven syllables. In this canzone only eleven-syllable lines are used.

The number of stanzas is optional. The " coda " or " envoi " preferably repeats some part of the stanza form.

In the later Provençal forms the stanzas were usually, though not always, more simple than this, and the rhymes of the first stanza were usually retained throughout the poem ; thus each succeeding stanza was an echo not only of the order but of the terminal sounds of the first.

An effect of one of Arnaut Daniel's canzoni is that of a chord struck repeatedly in crescendo. The sound-beauty of the Italian canzone depends on the variation of the rhymes.

The Provençal canzone can be understood when sung. Tuscan canzoni often require close study in print before they will yield their meaning. But after one knows the meaning, their exquisite sound spoken, or sung, is most enjoyable.

The following canzone is explained at length in the Convito.
It tells how Dante is led out from his personal grief for the
death of Beatrice into the sunlight of Philosophy ; that is,
becomes fit for his life work, because of a deepened vision.
It is addressed to the spirits, who, by understanding, rule the
third heaven—the heaven of Love—because they alone will
fully comprehend it. The speakers in the poem are : A spirit,
descending on the rays of Venus, the star ruling the third
heaven ; a thought that goes from Dante to heaven and returns
telling him of Beatrice, the " angiola " (little angel), who is
crowned in heaven ; the " spiritel " or breath of noble love :
and other speakers who are sufficiently explained in the text.[9]

Canzone Prima from Il Convito

Ye moving spirits of the third high sphere,
Hear ye this speech as in my heart it is !
Too strange it is to speak, save unto you.
That heaven which followeth your potencies
(O creatures noble as ye do appear)
Forms now the mood which I am drawn unto,
Wherefore this speech of life which I pass through,
Meseems directed toward you worthily.
And therefore I pray ye give me heed
While my heart speaks that which is new indeed,
Of how, within, my soul weeps piteously
Because a spirit borne upon the rays
Of your high star, my soul in speech withstays.

The life of my sad heart was wont to be
A gracious thought which many a time went thence
To take his place beside thy Sire's feet,
Where looked he on *her* gloried countenance,
Of whom he spoke to me so graciously,
That my soul cried : ' My going hence is meet.'
And now comes one who drives him in defeat,
And lords it over me with such high power
That my heart's trembling is made manifest.

[9] (I didn't know Shelley had translated it first.)

To make me look on her, this is his quest,
Who saith, 'Whoso would win salvation's dower,
Unto this lady let him turn his eyes,
If he may strip his fear of fearful sighs.

The humble thought which wont to speak to me
Of a little angel who in heaven is crowned,
Finds here a foe, who him destroyeth straight ;
And weeping saith my soul, in this grief bound,
' Alas ! that now that piteous one doth flee
Who gave me comforting until so late ! '
And of mine eyes he saith, disconsolate,
' Oimè ! what hour, wherein they saw her first !
Why trusted they not me concerning her ?
I ever said, within her eyes doth stir
A power whereby my peers to death are cursed.
What was my warning more than wasted breath,
They would not turn from her, from whom is my death ? '

' Thou art not dead, thou only art dismayed,
O soul of ours, who makest here such moan.'
A breath of noble love replies to this,
' For this fair lady who is here made known
Hath on thy life such transmutation laid
That fear comes on thee and strange cowardice.
How humble and how pitiful she is,
And in her grandure wise and courteous !
Behold, and know, and name her "Mistress" ever.
And hence, unless thy mind from sense him sever,
Thou shalt see glories, high, so marvelous,
That thou shalt cry, " Love, Lord in verity,
Behold thine handmaid ! Do what pleaseth thee ! " ' '

Canzon, I think that they shall be but few,
Who shall draw forth thy meaning rightfully,
So wearisome and tangled is thy speech,
Whence, if such fortune falleth unto thee,
That pathways of thy going shall lie through
Minds unto whom thy meaning can not reach,
Take thou such comfort as I here can teach :
Greet them, my New Delight, with this address,
' Give heed at least unto my loveliness.'[10]

[19] Ponete mente almen com' io son bella.

The cult of Provence had been a cult of the emotions ; and with it there had been some, hardly conscious, study of emotional psychology. In Tuscany the cult is a cult of the harmonies of the mind. If one is in sympathy with this form of objective imagination and this quality of vision, there is no poetry which has such enduring, such, if I may say so, indestructible charm.

The best poetry of this time appeals by its truth, by its subtlety, and by its refined exactness. Noffo Bonaguida thus expresses himself and the peculiar introspective tendency of his time :

> Ispirito d'Amor con intelletto
> Dentro dallo meo cor sempre dimora,
> Chi mi mantiene in gran gioia e'n diletto
> E senza lui non viveria un' ora.

Our whole appreciation of the time depends on whether we understand what is meant by the peculiar terms : thus in the above passage whether we mistranslate " intelletto " as " intellect," or render it correctly " intelligence," thus :

> A spirit of love with intelligence
> Dwells ever within my heart,
> He maintains me in joy and great delight,
> Without him I should die within the hour.

Faults this poetry may have ; we have already mentioned them at too great length ; this virtue it ever has, it is not rhetorical, it aims to be what it is, and never pretends to be something which it is not.

Seeking, in the works of the centuries immediately preceding him, those elements which Dante's magnanimity has welded into the *Commedia*, we find much of his philosophy or theology in the church fathers. Richard of St. Victor had written a prose which becomes poetry, not because of its floridity, but because of its intensity.

The technique of accented verse had been developed by Daniel, Guinicelli, and Cavalcanti.

In Rustico di Filippo we find proof that the bitter acid of Italian speech was not first distilled by the Florentine.

Lorris, Clopinel, and Brunetto Latini had already attempted long poems which were not romances or narratives of deed. St. Francis had poured out his religious fervor in the tongue of the people.   The means are prepared.

VII

Ignorance of most of the data of Dante's life is no bar to the understanding of his works.

The life itself is, however, most interesting, and Paget Toynbee has set down the main facts with such fluent conciseness that the information conveyed greatly exceeds the labor of reading.[1]

I have recommended few subsidiary works. I believe that in the study of literature one should read texts, not commentaries. I recommend the first 157 pages of Toynbee as a biographical introduction to Dante's *Commedia*.

Toynbee follows the sane custom of quoting contemporary authorities : Villari, etc., at reasonable length.

In outline the facts are these :

Dante was born in Florence in 1265 ; his father, Guelph, judge and notary. [Toynbee's characterization of Dante's father is, I think, drawn mainly from Mr. Toynbee's imagination, without any real warrant ascertained in facts ; however, the point is of no consequence ; our enjoyment of the *Commedia* does not depend on Alighiero degli Alighieri's views on vendetta.] Dante's mother was of Ghibelline family. The Ghibelline party, ruined in the year of Dante's birth, stood in theory for " law, authority, the empire, and the older aristocracy " ; the Guelph party for the citizens, the Church, liberty, and Italy.

The *Vita Nuova*, the prose of which was written between 1292–95, is Dante's own account of his youth's inner life, and we have Boccaccio and Dante's own son to witness that it tells of Dante's love for Beatrice Portinari.

On June 11, 1289, Dante fought at Campaldino, " in the front rank " " no child in arms " ; possibly among " the 150

[1] Paget Toynbee : *Life of Dante*.

of the best of the host," chosen by Aimeri of Narbonne and the other Florentine captains. The battle was between the Guelphs of Florence and the Ghibellines, who had for some years been centred at Arezzo. Dante saw further military service. In 1295-6 he enrolled himself in the Guild of Physicians and Apothecaries, which Guild was concerned with the trade with the Orient : spices, drugs, pearls, jewels, books, and the art of painting.

By 1298 he was married to Gemma Donati ; elected in 1300 to the priority of Florence, then torn by the Black and White factions of the Guelph party. For the peace of the city he exiled the leaders of both factions ; among them his friend, Guido Cavalcanti, who was shortly recalled, but died of a fever contracted in exile.

In 1301, when Pope Boniface attempted to interfere in the civic affairs of Florence, Dante and a few others were sent as ambassadors to Rome. During their absence the party of the Black Guelphs (headed by the relations of Dante's wife) admitted into Florence Charles of Valois, the Pope's instrument. The Whites were treacherously driven out, and a decree of exile passed against Dante and others.

The rest of Dante's life was passed in exile, with the Scaligers, the Malespina, and other noble families. He wandered through most of the cities of Italy ; perhaps even to Paris or Oxford.

He was engaged much of the time in intriguing for a recall to Florence, which never came to him. His last hope of it was extinguished by the death of the Emperor Henry VII in 1313, two years after he had assumed the iron crown of Milan and threatened Florence. The rest of Dante's life was passed in writing and in missions for his friends, such as the embassy to Venice for Guida da Polenta, on which he caught his death fever in 1321.

Toynbee's book, to which I have referred, is all the more remarkable for giving a lucid account of the party feuds in

Florence, and his account of Farinata degli Uberti is better than the notes on Farinata in most editions of the *Commedia*.

As for Dante's art, which is really what concerns us, we find him with a finished technique at twenty : presuming the second and fourth sonnets of the *Vita Nuova* to have been written about that time ; and it is in this ivory book of his youth that one should first come to know him. It opens thus :

I

In that part of the book of my memory, before which little can be read, is found a rubric, which saith, ' Beginneth the New Life.' Under the which rubric I find written the words which it is my intent to copy into this book, if not all, at least their meaning.

II

The heaven of light had revolved nine times in its orbit since my birth, when first appeared unto mine eyes the glorious lady of my mind, who was called Beatrice[2] by many who did not really understand what they called her.

In this fashion he begins the tale of Love the revealer, of Love the door and the way into the intelligence, of Love infinite " That moves the sun and all the other stars."

The narration is simple, without glare of incident ; the sight of Beatrice, the child, in a crimson mantle ; the sight of Beatrice, the lady, in white ; a greeting given smilingly, a greeting withheld ; the death of a friend they had in common ; the death of Folco Portinari, with presage of gloom impending, since the passing of these dim personalities in some sort foreshadows the death of Beatrice herself. We find not the action itself, but the action reflected in Dante's heart ; the heart, as we find it first, of one diffident, sensitive, somewhat bookish, a knower of dreams rather than a mixer among men. He is a master of frail harmonies almost from the beginning, in witness the second

[2] *Beatrice*—the blessed one.

sonnet and the fourth : sonnets by an older definition and more beautiful in form than the quatorzain.   The second begins :

> O voi che per la via d'Amor passate.
> O ye that pass along love's way.

And the fourth :

> Morte villana, di pieta nemica,
> Di dolor madre antica,
> Giudizio incontrastabile, gravoso,
> Poich' hai data materia al cor doglioso,
> Ond' io vado pensoso,
> Di te biasmar la lingua s' affatica.

Which Rossetti renders :

> Death, always cruel, Pity's foe in chief,
> Mother who brought forth grief,
> Merciless judgment and without appeal !
> Since thou alone hast made my heart to feel
> This sadness and unweal,
> My tongue upbraideth thee without relief.

Even Rossetti is unable to continue in the strict rime scheme of the original.   Perhaps the first flawless sonnet of the *Vita Nuova* is the fifth, " Cavalcando l'altr'ier per un camino," which is to be found in Rossetti's translation of *The New Life.*

From this point onward the tale is of visions, and of Love's lordship over the singer, until with the death of Beatrice comes the final refinement of the song.

Of his griefs before that time and after it, I would rather you read from the full text.   The *Vita Nuova* is not a thing to be pulled apart and illustrated by selections.   There are some thirty pages of it : songs and a quaint prose forming a sort of extended " razzo," or explanation of the songs and their causes.

One can cast no spell with disconnected bars of a Chopin nocturne.   The *Vita Nuova*, frail, delicate in its brief extent, would suffer too much from a like dissolution.   The atmosphere, so much its own, so little belonging to anything but itself, is too much desecrated by a pulling awry of the matter.

The whole must be given to those to whom Dante addresses the first canzone, that is to those " ch'avete intelletto d' amore."

In the tenth and eleventh sonnets we find that he has been reading Maximus Guido Guinicelli. The tenth begins :

> Love and the noble heart are both one thing ;
> E'en thus the sage in his " dittato " saith.

It is a philosophizing little sonnet of the older school. The eleventh also stands in accord with the tradition, and having little individuality, suffers little by being taken apart from the context.

> Within her eyes my Lady beareth Love,
> So making noble all she looketh on.
> Where she passeth, straight turneth everyone toward her;
> Her greeting putteth a trembling on the heart,
> So that a man lowers his shaken visage
> And sigheth for every fault he hath,
> Pride and anger flee before her.
> Aid me then, ladies, in her honoring !

> All sweetnesss, every humble thought
> Is born within the heart of whoever hears her speak ;
> Whence is he blest who first looketh on her ;
> What thing she is when she faintly smileth
> Can not be said nor even held in mind,
> It is so new and noble a miracle.

The slight though striking similarity of the eleventh line to the first line of a poem of Sappho's, translated by Catullus, is perhaps mere accident ; but the sequent similarity of thoughts is interesting.

The vision of Love and the flaming heart ; of love in the guise of a pilgrim, and of the little cloud, cannot be separated from the whole. One tries to recall Browning's verses on the drawing of an angel (in *One Word More*). Dante's prose of it may be rendered as follows :[3]

[3] *La Vita Nuova,* XXXV.

In that day, fulfilling the year wherein this lady was made citizen of the life eternal, I was sitting in a place, wherein remembering her, I was designing an angel upon certain tablets, and while I was at the drawing I turned my eyes and saw beside me men whom it was befitting to honor. They watched what I was making, and afterwards it was told me that they had been there some while without my being aware of it. Seeing them, I arose and said to them in greeting : " Another was with me, whence my thought."

When they were gone, I turned to my work, that is, the drawing of an angel's face, and doing this there came to me the thought of setting certain words in rime, as for annual of her. Then spoke I the sonnet, " Era Venuta."

The following passages should send anyone who reads them to the full text.

Canzone II

A very pitiful lady, very young,
Exceeding rich in human sympathies,
Stood by what time I clamored upon death,
And at the wild words wandering on my tongue,
And at the piteous look within mine eyes,
She was affrighted, . . .

Of the visions in that troubled sleep of his, the later stanza :

Then saw I many broken hinted sights,
In the uncertain state I stepped into
Me seemed to be I know not in what place,
Where ladies through the streets, like mournful lights,
Ran with loose hair, and eyes that frighten'd you
By their own terror, and a pale amaze :
The while, little by little, as I thought,
The sun ceased, and the stars began to gather,
And each wept at the other ;
And birds dropp'd in mid-flight out of the sky ;
And earth shook suddenly ;
And I was 'ware of one, hoarse and tired out,
Who ask'd of me : "Hast thou not heard it said ? . . .
Thy lady, she that was so fair, is dead."

The third canzone mourns likewise :

> That she hath gone to Heaven suddenly,
> And hath left love below to mourn with me.
>
> Beatrice is gone up into high Heaven,
> The kingdom where the angels are at peace :
> And lives with them ; and to her friends is dead.
> Not by the frost of winter was she driven
> Away, like others ; nor by summer heats ;
> But through a perfect gentleness, instead.
> For from the lamp of her meek lowlihead
> Such an exceeding glory went up hence
> That it woke wonder in the Eternal Sire,
> Until a sweet desire
> Enter'd Him for that lovely excellence,
> So that He bade her to Himself aspire ;
> Counting this weary and most evil place
> Unworthy of a thing so full of grace.

The conclusion of the *Vita Nuova*, which is also the prologue to the *Commedia*, runs thus in Rossetti's version :

About this time, it happened that a great number of persons undertook a pilgrimage, to the end that they might behold that blessed portraiture bequeathed unto us by our Lord Jesus Christ as the image of his beautiful countenance (upon which countenance my dear lady now looked continually.) And certain among these pilgrims, who seemed very thoughtful, passed by a path which is well-nigh in the midst of the city where my most gracious lady was born, and abode, and at last died.

Then I, beholding them, said within myself : These pilgrims seem to be come from very far ; and I think they can not have heard speak of this lady, or known anything concerning her. Their thoughts are not of her, but of other things ; it may be, of their friends who are far distant, and whom we, in our turn, know not. . . . And when the last of them had gone by me, I bethought me to write a sonnet, showing forth mine inward speech. . . . And I wrote this sonnet :

> Ye pilgrim folk advancing pensively
> As if in thought of distant things, I pray,
> Is your own land indeed so far away
> As by your aspect it would seem to be,—

That nothing of our grief comes over ye
Though passing through the mournful town midway ;
Like unto men that understand today
Nothing at all of her great misery ?
Yet if ye will but stay, whom I accost,
And listen to my words a little space,
At going ye shall mourn with a loud voice.
It is her Beatrice that she hath lost ;
Of whom the least word spoken holds such grace
That men weep hearing it, and have no choice.

And I . . . resolved that I would write also a new thing, . . . therefore I made this sonnet, which narrates my condition, . . .

Beyond the sphere which spreads to widest space
Now soars the sigh that my heart sends above :
A new perception born of grieving love
Guideth it upward through the untrodden ways.
When it hath reach'd the end, and stays,
It sees a lady round whom splendors move
In homage ; till, by the great light thereof
Abash'd, the pilgrim spirit stands at gaze.
It sees her such, that when it tells me this
Which it hath seen, I understand it not,
It hath a speech so subtle and so fine,
And yet I know its voice within my thought
Often remembereth me of Beatrice :
So that I understand it, ladies mine.

After writing this sonnet, it was given unto me to behold a very wonderful vision ; wherein I saw things which determined me that I would say nothing further of this most blessed one, until such time as I could discourse more worthily concerning her. And to this end I labor all I can, as she well knoweth. Wherefore if it be His pleasure through whom is the life of all things, that my life continue with me a few years, it is my hope that I shall yet write concerning her what hath not before been written of any woman. After the which, may it seem good unto Him who is the Master of Grace, that my spirit should go hence to behold the glory of its lady, to wit, of that blessed Beatrice who now gazeth continually on His countenance *qui est per omnia sæcula benedictus*. Laus Deo.

Thus ends the ivory book he sent to Ser Brunetto.

Saving the grace of a greatly honored scholar, to speak of the *Vita Nuova* as " embroidered with conceits " is arrant nonsense. The *Vita Nuova* is strangely unadorned ; more especially is this evident if it be compared with work of its own date. It is without strange, strained similes.

Anyone who has in any degree the faculty of vision will know that the so-called personifications are real and not artificial. Dante's precision both in the *Vita Nuova* and in the *Commedia* comes from the attempt to reproduce exactly the thing which has been clearly seen. The " Lord of terrible aspect " is no abstraction, no figure of speech. There are some who can not or will not understand these things. For such let Dante's own words suffice. They are to be found in one of those passages of explanation which must have seemed to the author so prolix, so unnecessary. Thus :

Nevertheless, he who is not of wit sufficient to understand it (Canzone prima) by these (explanations) which have already been made, is welcome to leave it alone.

That the *Vita Nuova* is the idealization of a real woman can be doubted by no one who has, even in the least degree, that sort of intelligence whereby it was written, or who has known in any degree the passion whereof it treats.[4]

Out of the wonderful vision mentioned in the last passage quoted sprang the *Commedia* ; and it is to this passage that Cino da Pistoija refers in that sonnet ending, " Sing on till thou redeem thy plighted word," a sonnet probably written after *The Inferno* had been begun, and sent to the exiled Dante, who had ceased from his making.

[4] 1929 : One is less emphatic twenty years later and less certain just what passion is implied, or one is, at least, less vigorous about those who held an opposite view.

THE COMMEDIA

The *Commedia*, as Dante has explained in the Epistle to Can Grande, is written in four senses : the literal, the allegorical, the anagogical, and the ethical. For this form of arcana we find the best parallel in the expressions of mathematics. Thus, when we are able to see that one general law governs such a series of equations as $3 \times 3 + 4 \times 4 = 5 \times 5$, or written more simply, $3^2 + 4^2 = 5^2$, $6^2 + 8^2 = 10^2$, $12^2 + 16^2 = 20^2$, etc., express the common relation algebraically $a^2 + b^2 = c^2$. When one has learned common and analytical geometry, one understands that this relation, $a^2 + b^2 = c^2$, exists between two sides of the right angle triangle and its hypotenuse, and that likewise in analytics for the points forming the circumference of any circle. Thus to the trained mathematician the cryptic $a^2 + b^2 = c^2$ expresses :

1st. A series of abstract numbers in a certain relation to each other.

2nd. A relation between certain abstract numbers.

3rd. The relative dimensions of a figure ; in this case a triangle.

4th. The idea or ideal of the circle.

Thus the *Commedia* is, in the literal sense, a description of Dante's vision of a journey through the realms inhabited by the spirits of men after death ; in a further sense it is the journey of Dante's intelligence through the states of mind wherein dwell all sorts and conditions of men before death ; beyond this, Dante or Dante's intelligence may come to mean " Everyman " or " Mankind," whereat his journey becomes a symbol of mankind's struggle upward out of ignorance into the clear light of philosophy. In the second sense I give here, the journey is Dante's own mental and spiritual development. In a fourth sense, the *Commedia* is an expression of the laws of eternal justice ; " il contrapasso," the counterpass, as Bertran calls it[5] or the law of Karma, if we are to use an Oriental term.

[5] *Inferno*, XXIV.

THE SPIRIT OF ROMANCE

Every great work of art owes its greatness to some such complexity. Thus *Hamlet* is a great play, not because it narrates the misventures of an introspective prince of Denmark, but because every man reading it finds something of himself in Hamlet. The play is also an enunciation to the effect that a man's thoughts or dreams

> " Come between him and the deed of his hand,
> Come between him and the hope of his heart."

There is little doubt that Dante conceived the real Hell, Purgatory, and Paradise as states, and not places. Richard St. Victor had, somewhile before, voiced this belief, and it is, moreover, a part of the esoteric and mystic dogma. For the purposes of art and popular religion it is more convenient to deal with such matters objectively ; this also was most natural in an age wherein it was the poetic convention to personify abstractions, thoughts, and the spirits of the eyes and senses, and indeed nearly everything that could be regarded as an object, an essence, or a quality. It is therefore expedient in reading the *Commedia* to regard Dante's descriptions of the actions and conditions of the shades as descriptions of men's mental states in life, in which they are, after death, compelled to continue : that is to say, men's inner selves stand visibly before the eyes of Dante's intellect, which is guided by a personification of classic learning, mystic theology, and the beneficent powers.

The journey of the vision begins in a thick forest midway along life's road, whence Dante, in fear of certain symbolical beasts, is led by Virgil through and out of Hell, and to the summit of Purgatory, where another guide awaits to accompany him out through the concentric spheres of the heavens into unbounded heaven above them.

One hears far too much about Dante's *Hell*, and far too little about the poetry of the *Purgatorio* and *Paradiso* ; though Dante has warned his readers in the ninth line of the first canto, that the *Hell* is but the prelude :

> Ma per trattar del ben ch'io vi trovai,
> Dirò dell' altre cose ch'io v'ho scorte.

But to tell of the *good* which I found, I will speak also of the other things.

In the construction of the great symphony the first movement is sombre, only to make the last by contrast more luminous.

Guided by Virgil, Dante begins his descent into the conical pit, through ever-narrowing circles, and air ever more black and more tempestuous.

Hell is the state of man dominated by his passions ; who has lost " the good of the intelligence."[6]

First we come beneath the starless air to those dreary spirits who lacked energy to sin or to do good ; fit neither for Hell nor Heaven.

Next, to the ferry of Charon, where, " as the leaves of autumn fall one after one until the bough sees all its pageantry upon the earth, even so the evil seed of Adam cast themselves from the shore," into the barge of the red-eyed Charon.

Across the " livid marsh " Dante is taken in a swoon, into the place, " not sad with torments, but with shadows only," and here he meets the four other great poets, as his time knew them—Sovran Homer, Horace the satirist, Ovid and Lucan, who greet him and return with him and Virgil into the noble castle, " to the meadows of fresh verdure." It is the Hellenic Elysium, and in his description of it, Dante, I think, displays a certain quality of calm power, allegedly denied all authors save the Greek.

Drawing to one side, " into a place, open, luminous, and high," whence he could see all these " with slow eyes and grave, and of great authority in their semblance, speaking

[6] Che hanno perduto il ben del intelleto.

seldom, and with quiet ("soave") voices"; great spirits whom he gloried within him to have seen : "Elektra, Hector and Aeneas, and Cæsar with his falcon eyes ; Penthesilea, and Brutus, that drove forth Tarquin ; Camilla and Martia," and "by himself apart," the Saladin ; and higher, "the master of those that know,"[7] holding his Olympian Court with Plato and Socrates, Thales, and the rest.

Then the four poets leave Dante alone with Virgil, and "out from the calm air" they move "into the air which trembleth," "to a place where nothing shineth."

Minos, "knower of sins," reigns over it, and judges. In the "dolorous hospice," "where all light is mute, there is a bellowing as of the sea in tempest, of a storm that never rests." Whirling and smiting, the infernal wind beats here upon the spirits of those who were ruled by their own ungoverned emotions ; and as cranes go chanting their lays in a line long drawn through the air, so come there wailing ghosts, "As shadows borne upon th' aforesaid strife."[8]

And here (Canto V) Francesca da Rimini, one of the pair "that seemed so light upon the wind,[9] as one that speaks and weepeth," tells her tale of how there, "where the Po descendeth to be at peace with his attendant streams," "Love that the noble heart learneth quickly had joined her to one who leaves her never."

From the miraculous fifth canto the vision leads into new torments, through the circles of the gluttonous, and the avaricious, and the prodigal ; to the wrathful and the sullen, buried in the ooze of their sullenness. Over their pool Dante and Virgil come to the city of Dis, livid, with the walls of seeming iron ; place of the fallen angels, "basso inferno" ; place of the blood-stained Erynnis, girt with greenest hydras, coifed with serpents and cerastes. The præfects of the city refuse to

[7] Aristotle.
[8] Ombre portate della detta briga.
[9] E paion si al vento esser leggieri.

open to the poets, but their "fatal going" ("fatal andare")
is not to be impeded.

As at Arles, where the Rhone pools itself, as at Pola near the Quarnaro
gulf, which shuts up Italy and bathes its confines,
the sepulchres make all the place uneven : so did they here on every
side, only the manner here was more bitter :
for amongst the tombs were scattered flames. . . .
And I : 'Master, what are these people who, buried within those
chests, make themselves heard by their painful sighs ?'
And he to me : '[Here] are the Arch-heretics with their followers
of every sect ; and much more, than thou thinkest, the tombs
are laden.
Like with like is buried here ; and the monuments are more and
less hot.' [10]

Out of one of these fiery coffers rises Farinata degli Uberti,
agnostic, he who, after the battle of Arbia, had saved the city
of Florence from destruction at the hands of the Ghibelline
Council.

"As if he held hell in great disdain,"[11] he rises from his torture
to a combat of wits with his political enemy.

Past him and his tomb-mate, Guido Cavalcanti's father, the
two poets descend to the thicker stench of that part of Hell
reserved for the violent against themselves, against God, and
against their neighbors ; for blasphemers against God, and
despisers of nature's bounty : for the practisers of fraud against
those who have had, and against those who had not had
confidence in them ; until at the narrow base of hell we
find Judas, Brutus, and Cassius eternally embedded in the ice,
which is the symbol of the treacherous heart.

Beneath the reek of the lurid air, over rivers of blood, guarded
by monsters from the classic mythology, he shows us the world,
blind with its ignorance, its violence, and its filth.

[10] The translations of the *Commedia* quoted in this chapter are mostly those of
the Temple edition.
[11] Come avesse lo inferno in gran dispitto.

Browning is perhaps the only widely read modern who has realized this phase of the Middle Ages, and he has hidden his knowledge in an unread poem, *Sordello*.

The vigor of Browning's touch approaches the Florentine's in one passage at least, of Cino at the fountain, in the poem *Sordello* :

> ' A sort of Guelf folk gazed
> And laughed apart ; Cino disliked their air—
> Must pluck up spirit, show he does not care—
> Seats himself on the tank's edge—will begin
> To hum, *za, za, Cavaler Ecclin*—
> A silence ; he gets warmer, clinks to chime,
> Now both feet plough the ground, deeper each time,
> At last, *za, za*, and up with a fierce kick
> Comes his own mother's face, caught by the thick
> Grey hair about his spur ! '
>   Which means, they lift
> The covering, Salinguerra made a shift
> To stretch upon the truth ; as well avoid
> Further disclosures ; leave them thus employed.[12]

Piere Cardinal's fable of the sane man in the city gone mad is a weaker equation for what Dante presents as a living man amongst the dead.

I have followed convention in noting Farinata ; under the rain of dilated flakes of fire we find Capanæus, a like figure, unrelenting in his defiance of the supreme power :[13]

---

[12] 1929 : Dante is less in advance of his time than Guido Cavalcanti, but the Anglo-American perception, possibly the whole universitaire perception of mediaeval literature is distorted by neglect of Mussato. Mussato wrote in Latin and is therefore omitted from " courses." Browning had, I think indubitably, seen the *Ecerinus* ; at any rate that play will adjust one's focus. Mussato was crowned in his own day and gives certainly better indication of the general state of the mediaeval mind than anything we are likely to get from the highbrows of the period. The Italian translation by Dazzi is useful for those who read Italian and not Latin. *L'Ecerinide* di Alberto Mussato, tradotta da Manlio Torquato Dazzi, Casa Lapi, Citta di Castello, 1914.

[13] *Inferno*, XIV, 50.

What I was living that am I dead
Though Jove outweary his smith.

In Canto XV we find Brunetto Latini still anxious for the
literary immortality of his *Tesoro*.

Canto XVII opens with this description of Geryon, symbol
of fraud :

> Ecco la fiera con la coda aguzza
> Che passa i monti, e rompe muri e l'armi.

Behold the wild brute with sharpened tail that passeth mountains
and breaks walls and arms. Behold the one that fouleth all the world.
Thus began my guide to speak to me, and beckoned to the beast to
come to shore, near to the end of the rocky defile. And that uncleanly
image of fraud came on, and landed with head and breast. But drew
not its tail upon the bank. The face was the face of a just man, so
benign was the outer skin ; and the rest was all a serpent's body.
Two paws had he hairy to the armpits ; the back and the breast and
both the flanks he had mottled with knobs and circlets.
Never did Tartars or Turks weave cloth with more colors and
broidery, nor were such webs laid by Arachne.
As at times wherries lie ashore, that are part in water and part on
land ; and as there amongst the guzzling Germans[14] the beaver adjusts
himself to wage his war : so lay that worst of savage beasts upon the
brim."

They climb onto the back of this animal and descend into
the lower pit, "Malebolge," which contains the violent against
art, and the usurers. In this canto Dante attacks the " unearned
increment."

Geryon goes swimming slowly, slowly, wheels and descends ;
but I perceive it not, save by a wind upon my face and from below.

" Malebolge " is a series of concentric pits, the whole shaped
somewhat like a half-opened telescope. Through the *Inferno*
there is a biting satire on the aimless turmoil and restlessness of

[14] Tedeschi lurchi.

humanity, beginning with the motion of the wind which bears Paolo and Francesca, continuing through the portrayal of the devil-driven pandars in " Malebolge," only at the very root of Hell do we find the end of it, in the still malignity of the traitor's wallow.

Canto XIX is devoted to the simonists ; here Dante finds Nicholas III, to whom :

'O whoe'er thou art that hast thy upper part undermost, wretched spirit, planted like a stake,' I began, 'if thou art able, speak !'
I stood like a friar who is confessing a faithless assassin, who, after being planted, is thus recalled, and has his death delayed.
And he cried out : 'Art thou already standing, Boniface ?[15] Art thou already on end, Boniface ? The script has lied to me by several years.

Dante also anticipates the descent of Clement V to the same department, and inveighs against simony. There is a similar boldness shown by Guido Reni in his picture of St. Michael and the Devil, where the Devil's face is that of the Pope. In the further lines (121-124) we have hidden much of the spirit of the Renaissance. Dante here represents intelligence and truth, and Virgil the honesty of pagan philosophy ; at the end of Dante's invective he says of Virgil :

I believe, indeed, that this pleased my guide, with such contented lips did he listen to the sound of the words truly spoken.

It is said that Rabelais hid his wisdom in a mass of filth in order that it might be acceptable to his age ; Dante rather tactfully invokes pagan enlightenment to rebuke the corruption of the Church in a way that will not stir up the rabble.

When Dante weeps in pity for the sorcerers and diviners,[16] Virgil shows classic stoicism :

[15] Pope Boniface VIII.
[16] *Inferno*, XX.

Art thou, too, like the other fools ? Here liveth pity when it were well dead. Who is more impious than he who sorrows at divine judgment ?

Here the damned " made breasts of their shoulders because they wished to see too far before them."

Dante's love of beauty draws it after him into Hell itself, and he relieves the gloom of the canto by retrospection :

That is Aruns, who hath his belly behind him, he who, in the mountains of Luni, where hoes the Carrarese who dwells below, had his grotto amidst the white marbles and dwelt therein, and thence with unobstructed sight looked forth upon the stars and on the sea.

In the next cantos are scourged sins and the cities noted for them. Thus the barrators are " the elders of San Zita " (patron saint of Lucca). In Canto XXI (7-18 lines) is this simile so apt in its suggestion, of things marine.

As in the Venetians' arsenal boils the sticky pitch, for the caulking of damaged keels unnavigable, in which, to save rebuilding, they plug the ribs so that they hold for many a voyage ; while some hammer at the prow, some at the stern ; some make oars, others twine ropes, and mend the jib or mainsail, so, not by fire but by divine means, there is boiled down there a thick tar which glues the bank in every place.

Here are the barrators—the simile may seem overlong— but it also conveys that air of unrest, here the racket of the ship-yard.

There is grim humor through these canti. Bologna is gibed for pandars, as Lucca for barrators. Through it all moves Dante (a more impersonal figure than he is usually accounted), with his clear perception of evil and of pompous stupidity ; and his skill in giving " relief" from the mood of the *Inferno*, once as by the memory of Aruns' cave, next by the clearly comic touch of the infernal corporal, lord over four under-devils, who is the equivalent of the operatic " super " with a spear.

We lose a great deal if we leave our sense of irony behind us when we enter the dolorous ports of Dante's *Hell*. For sheer dreariness one reads Henry James, not the *Inferno*.

In the circle below the barrators go the hypocrites, clothed in great gilded mantles which are lined with lead ; the " painted people " weighed down with splendid appearances ; Caiaphas and Fra Catalano. With a grim reminder that Frederic of Sicily had made lead coats in which to roast a few traitors, or embezzlers of imperial funds.

Canto XXIV opens with the long simile of the peasant coming to his door : " When the hoar-frost paints her white sister's image on the ground."

This canto is of the thieves tormented by serpents, and Dante's sting is for Pistoija.

In XXVI, Florence is under the lash :

> Godi, Fiorenza, poi che sei si grande
> che per mare e per terra batti l'ali
> e per l'inferno il tuo nome si spande.

> Exult, O Florence, that art grown so grand,
> that over sea and land dost beat thy wings,
> e'en through th' inferno doth thy name expand.

Then, as the peasant who at the sun's hiding sees his valley filled with fire-flies, so Dante, looking down across this Hell-ditch, sees approaching that multitude of flames which involves each one, one evil councillor.

The punishment of the sowers of discord I have mentioned in the paragraphs on Bertrans de Born. Below them are the rebellious giants, and lastly the traitors in the circle of ice, and with them the " emperor of the dolorous realm " tri-faced, the very core of Hell. Clambering over his shaggy bulk, Dante and Virgil enter the " cammino ascoso," the hidden road, and by this ascent issue forth to see again the stars.[17]

---

[17] E quindi uscimmo a riveder le stelle.

The Purgatorio

To course o'er better waters now hoists sail the little bark of my wit,
leaving behind her so cruel a sea.

And I will sing of that second realm, where the human spirit is purged,
and becomes worthy to ascend to Heaven.

But here let dead poesy arise again, O holy muses, since yours am I ;
and here let Calliope arise somewhat,

accompanying my song with that strain whose stroke the wretched
Pies felt so that they despaired of pardon.

The sweet color of oriental sapphire which was gathering on the serene
aspect of the pure air even to the first circle,

to mine eyes restored delight, as soon as I issued forth from the dead
air, which had afflicted eyes and heart.

The fair planet which heartenest to love was making the whole East
to laugh, veiling the Fishes that were in her train.

Thus opens the second great division of the *Commedia*. Cato
challenges their progress ; then follows the description of the
angelic steersman.[18]

We were alongside the ocean yet, like folk who ponder o'er their road,
who go in heart and in body stay ;

as on the approach of morning, through the dense mists Mars burns
red, low in the West o'er the ocean-floor ;

such to me appeared—so may I see it again !—a light coming o'er
the sea so swiftly, that no flight is equal to its motion ;

from which, when I had a while withdrawn mine eyes to question
my Leader, I saw it brighter and larger grown.

Then on each side of it appeared to me something white ; and from
beneath it, little by little, another whiteness came forth.

My Master yet spake no word, until the first whiteness appeared as
wings ; then, when well he knew the pilot,

he cried : Bend, bend thy knees ; behold the Angel of God : fold
thy hands : henceforth shalt thou see such ministers.

Look how he scorns all human instruments, so that oar he wills not,
nor other sail than his wings, between shores so distant.

See how he has them heavenward turned, plying the air with eternal
plumes, that are not moulted like mortal feathers.

Then as more and more towards us came the bird divine, brighter
yet he appeared, wherefore mine eye endured him not near :

[18] *Purgatorio*, II, 10–45.

but I bent it down, and he came on to the shore with a vessel so swift
and light that the waters nowise drew it in.
On the stern stood the celestial pilot, such, that blessedness seemed
writ upon him, and more than a hundred spirits sat within."

Among the souls is Casella, musician of Florence, who
explains how the souls are conveyed to the Holy Mount, from
that "shore where the Tiber's waves turn salt." He sings for
memory's sake, creating yet another memory, "Amor che
nella mente mi ragiona," the Dantescan ode for which presumably, in the time of their early friendship, he had made
the "Son" or tune.

Ascending the hard way, they meet Manfred among the
excommunicated, Belacqua among the late repentant, and
among the late repentant violently slain, Buonconte and others ;
beyond them is Sordello, alone in the valley of Princes. The
day ends ; "Te lucis ante" is sung. Two angels descend.

Green, as tender leaves just born, was their raiment, which they
trailed behind, fanned and smitten by green wings.[19]

Sordello continues his explanation of the place, and the ante-
purgatory. Canto IX brings us to the gate of Purgatory proper.
The seven terraces for the purgation of Pride, Envy, Anger,
Sloth, Avarice and Prodigality, Gluttony and Lust are guarded
at their entrances by the angels of the antithetic virtues ; above
them is the earthly Paradise.

It is possible that the figures in the *Purgatorio* are less vigorous
than those in the *Inferno*, and that Dante, in this middle realm,
permits himself too much luxury of explanation. For the
mystic, the *Paradiso* overwhelms it. For the lover of poetry,
however, the last six canti, describing the Earthly Paradise,
makes the second book not the least of the three. I do not
wish to slight the preceding canti, but they are overshadowed
by the magnificence of a conclusion which it is almost impossible
to convey, except by longish quotations.

[19] *Purgatorio*, VIII, 28–30.

Canto XXVIII

Now eager to search within and around the divine forest dense
and verdant, which to mine eyes was tempering the new day,

without waiting more I left the mountain-side, crossing the plain with
lingering step, over the ground which gives forth fragrance on every
side.

A sweet air, itself invariable, was striking on my brow with no greater
force than a gentle wind,

before which the branches, responsively trembling, were all bending
towards that quarter, where the holy mount casts its first shadow ;

yet not so far bent aside from their erect state, that the little birds
in the tops ceased to practise their every art ;

but, singing, with full gladness they welcomed the first breezes within
the leaves, which were murmuring the burden to their songs ;

even such as from bough to bough is gathered through the pine wood
on Chiassi's shore, when Aeolus looses Sirocco forth.

Already my slow steps had carried me on so far within the ancient
wood, that I could not see whence I had entered ;

and lo, a stream took from me further passage which, toward the left
with its little waves, bent the grass which sprang forth on its bank.

All the waters which here are purest, would seem to have some mixture
in them, compared with that, which hideth nought ;

albeit full darkly it flows beneath the everlasting shade, which never
lets sun, nor moon, beam there.

With feet I halted and with mine eyes did pass beyond the rivulet,
to gaze upon the great diversity of the tender blossoms ;

and there to me appeared, even as on a sudden something appears which,
through amazement, sets all other thought astray,

a lady solitary, who went along singing, and culling flower after
flower, wherewith all her path was painted.

Pray, fair lady, who at love's beams dost warm thee, if I may believe
outward looks, which are wont to be a witness of the heart,

may it please thee to draw forward, said I to her, towards this stream,
so far that I may understand what thou singest.

Thou makest me to remember, where and what Proserpine was in the
time her mother lost her, and she the spring.

As a lady who is dancing turns her round with feet close to the ground
and to each other, and hardly putteth foot before foot,

she turned toward me upon the red and upon the yellow flowerets,
not otherwise than a virgin that droppeth her modest eyes ;

and satisfied my prayer, drawing so near that the sweet sound reached
    me with its meaning.

Soon as she was there, where the grass is already bathed by the waves
    of the fair river, she vouchsafed to raise her eyes to me.

I do not believe that so bright a light shone forth under the eyelids of
    Venus, pierced by her son, against all his wont.

She smiled from the right bank opposite, gathering more flowers with
    her hands, which the high land bears without seed.

Three paces the river kept us distant ; but Hellespont, where Xerxes
    crossed, to this day a curb to all human pride,

endured not more hatred from Leander for its turbulent waves 'twixt
    Sestos and Abydos, than that did from me, because it opened
    not then.

The symbolic pageant appears, the light of seven candlesticks
is swept back above a car drawn by the grifon.

The pageant moves eastward ; Dante beholds the mystic
tree. The vision is filled with a profusion of symbols, as bewil-
dering as those in Ezekiel ; Dante, having drunk of Lethe and
Eunoe, concludes the *Purgatorio* :

> I came back from the most holy waves born again, even as new trees
> renewed with new foliage, pure and ready to mount to the stars.[20]

THE PARADISO

" The colorless and formless and intangible essence is visible
to the mind, which is the only lord of the soul : circling around
this in the region above the heavens is the place of true knowledge." Thus Plato in the *Phædrus* ; and likewise, " Now of
the heaven which is above the heavens no earthly poet has
sung, or ever will sing in a worthy manner."

Here our agreement with Plato is to be tempered by the
definition of two words : undefined " earthly " and " worthy."
Yet if we seek a true definition of the *Paradiso* we must take it
from the same Greek dialogue :

And this is the recollection of those things which our souls

[20] Puro e disposto a salire alle stelle. *Purgatorio*, XXXIII, 142–5.

saw when in company with God—when looking down from above on that which we now call being, and upward toward the true being.

In Canto I of the *Paradiso* we find :

The All-mover's glory penetrates through the universe, and regloweth in one region more, and less in another.
In that heaven which most receiveth of his light have I been ; and have seen things which whoso descendeth from up there hath neither knowledge nor power to re-tell ;
because, as it draweth nigh to its desire, our intellect sinketh so deep that memory cannot go back upon the track.
Natheless, whatever of the holy realm I had the power to treasure in my memory shall now be matter of my song.

Nowhere is the nature of the mystic ecstasy so well described here :

" Gazing on her such I became within, as was Glaucus, tasting of the grass that made him the sea-fellow of the other gods."

Yet there follows the reservation in the next lines :

To pass beyond humanity may not be told in words, wherefore let the example satisfy him for whom grace reserveth the experience.
If I was only that of me which thou didst new-create, O Love who rulest heaven, thou knowest, who with thy light didst lift me up.
When the wheel which thou, by being longed for, makest eternal, drew unto itself my mind with the harmony which thou dost temper and distinguish,
so much of heaven then seemed to me enkindled with the sun's flame, that rain nor river ever made a lake so widely distended.

Dante's own attitude towards the readers of his highest song is everywhere manifest.

Beatrice's gentleness in guiding him: [21]

Whereon she, after a sigh of pity, turned her eyes toward me with that look a mother casts on her delirious child ;
and began : ' All things whatsoever observe a mutual order ; and this is the form that maketh the universe like unto God.'

[21] *Paradiso*, I, 100–105.

is in some measure extended to the reader, who is both warned and allured :[22]

> O ye who in your little skiff, longing to hear, have followed on my keel that singeth on its way,
> turn to revisit your own shores ; commit you not to the open sea ; for perchance, losing me, ye would be left astray.
> The water which I take was never coursed before ; Minerva bloweth, Apollo guideth me, and the nine Muses point me to the Bears.
> Ye other few, who timely have lifted up your necks for bread of angels whereby life is here sustained but wherefrom none cometh away sated,
> ye may indeed commit your vessel to the deep keeping my furrow, in advance of the water that is falling back to the level.
> The glorious ones who fared to Colchis not so marvelled as shall ye, when Jason turned ox-ploughman in their sight.
> The thirst, born with us and ne'er failing, for the god-like realm bore us swift almost as ye see the heaven.

For the description of the ascent the following passages serve without gloze :[23]

> Meseemed a cloud enveloped us, shining dense, firm and polished like diamond smitten by the sun.
> Within itself the eternal pearl received us, as water doth receive a ray of light, though still itself uncleft.

With such beauty as this is the *Paradiso* radiant. Thus of the spirits in the lunar heaven :[24]

> In such guise as, from glasses transparent and polished, or from waters clear and tranquil, not so deep that the bottom is darkened,
> come back the notes of our faces, so faint that a pearl on a white brow cometh not slowlier, upon our pupils ;
> so did I behold many a countenance, eager to speak ; wherefore I fell into the counter-error of that which kindled love between the man and fountain.
> No sooner was I aware of them, thinking them reflected images, I turned round my eyes to see of whom they were.

[22] *Paradiso*, II, 1–21.
[23] *Paradiso*, II, 31–6.
[24] *Paradiso*, III, 9–24.

Picarda's speech of explanation contains that philosophy with which some say the poem is overloaded. Surely this also is the very marrow of beauty.[25]

'Brother, the quality of love stilleth our will, and maketh us long only for what we have, and giveth us no other thirst.

Did we desire to be more aloft, our longings were discordant from his will who here assorteth us,

and for that, thou wilt see, there is no room within these circles, if of necessity we have our being here in love, and if thou think again what is love's nature.

Nay, 'tis the essence of this blessed being to hold ourselves within the divine will, whereby our own wills are themselves made one.

So that our being thus, from threshold unto threshold throughout the realm, is a joy to all the realm as to the king, who draweth our wills to what he willeth ;

and his will is our peace ; it is that sea to which all moves that it createth and that nature maketh.'

Clear was it then to me how everywhere in heaven is Paradise, e'en though the grace of the chief Good doth not reign there after one fashion only.

The beauty of the *Paradiso* hardly suffers one to transplant it in fragments, as I here attempt.

It is of this sort of poetry that Coleridge says : " Our regard is not for particular passages but for a continuous undercurrent." There are beautiful images in the *Paradiso*, but the chief marvel is not the ornament. Such lines as these :[26]

> Io veggio ben si come gia risplende
> Nello intelletto tuo l'eterna luce,
> Che, vista sola, sempre amore accende ;
>
> E s' altra cosa vostro amor seduce,
> Non è se non di quella alcun vestigio
> Mal conosciuto, che quivi traluce

lose too much in a prose translation, illuminated though they be in essence.

[25] *Paradiso*, III, 70–91.
[26] *Paradiso*, V, 7–12.

In Canto VI the incident of Romeo can be disentangled from its context. We are now in the heaven of mercury, the second heaven, assigned to the honor-seeking.

Divers voices upon earth make sweet melody, and so the divers seats
    in our life render sweet harmony amongst these wheels.
And within the present pearl shineth the light of Romeo, whose
    beauteous and great work was so ill answered.
But the Provençals who wrought against him have not the laugh ;
    wherefore he taketh an ill path who maketh of another's good
    work his own loss.
Four daughters had Raymond Berenger, and every one a queen, and
    this was wrought for him by Romeo, a lowly and an alien man ;
then words uttered askance moved him to demand account of this
    just man, who gave him five and seven for every ten ;
who then took his way in poverty and age ; and might the world know
    the heart he had within him, begging his life by crust and crust,
    much as it praiseth, it would praise him more.

The historical background to the passage can be found in " Villani," or in the notes to the Temple edition of the *Paradiso*.

Though it be true that no man who has not passed through, or nearly approached that spiritual experience known as illumination—I use the word in a technical sense—can appreciate the *Paradiso* to the full, yet there is sheer poetic magic in a line like,[27] " Gli angeli, frate, e il paese sincero."

I am always filled with a sort of angry wonder that any one professing to care for poetry can remain in ignorance of the tongue in which the poem is written. It shows a dulness, a stolidity, which is incomprehensible to any one who knows the *Commedia*.

I do not need to quote the subtlest living translator, who, speaking of the still unsurpassed vision of *The Divine Comedy*, says : " To translate Dante is an impossible thing, for to do it would demand, as the *first* requirement, a *concise* and *luminous* style equal to Wordsworth at his *best*." The italics are my own ;

[27] *Paradiso*, VII, 130.

the quotation is from Arthur Symons, on Cary, in *The Romantic Movement in English Literature*.

The original of the following passage[28]

> Creata fu la *materia* ch' egli hanno,
> creata fu la virtù informante
> in queste stelle, che intorno a lor vanno.
>
> L' anima d' ogni bruto e delle piante
> di complession potenziata tira
> lo raggio e il moto delle luci sante.
>
> Ma vostra vita senza mezzo spira
> la somma beninanza, e la innamora
> di sè, si poi sempre la disira,

is infinitely more beautiful than the bare sense in English, which is :

Created was the matter which they hold, created was the informing virtue in these stars which sweep around them.

The life of every brute and of the plants is drawn from compounds having potency, by the ray and movement of the sacred lights.

But your life is breathed without mean by the supreme beneficence who maketh it enamoured of itself,[29] so that thereafter it doth ever long for it.

> In queste stelle, che intorno a lor vanno,

with the suave blending of the elided vowels, has in its sound alone more of the serene peace from that unsullied country than can be conveyed in any words save those flowing from the lips of a supreme genius.

Canto VIII, 13–27

I had no sense of rising into it, but my lady gave me full faith that I was there, because I saw her grow more beautiful.

And as we see a spark within a flame, and as a voice within a voice may be distinguished, if one stayeth firm, and the other cometh and goeth ;

[28] *Paradiso*, VII, 136–144.
[29] i.e. the beneficence.

so, in that light itself I perceived other torches moving in a circle more
or less swift, after the measure, I suppose, of their eternal vision.
From a chill cloud there ne'er descended blasts, or visible or no, so
rapidly as not to seem hindered and lagging.
to whomso should have seen those lights divine advance towards us,
quitting the circling that hath its first beginning in the exalted
Seraphim.

He is speaking of the third heaven, that of Venus.
Here, in defiance of convention, we find Cunizza :[30]

Out of one root spring I with it ; Cunizza was I called, and here I
glow because the light of this star overcame me.

In Canto IX, lines 103–106,

Yet here we not repent, but smile ; not at the sin, which cometh
not again to mind, but at the Worth that ordered and provided,

we have matter for a philosophical treatise as long as the
Paradiso.   Canto IX, lines 133–135,

Therefore it is that the Gospel and great Doctors are deserted, and
only the Decretals are so studied, as may be seen upon their
margins,

shows Dante's scant regard for the ecclesiastical lumber by which
his philosophy is said by certain critics to be smothered.
With the third heaven the shadow of earth is left behind ;
in the fourth, the shadow of the sun :[31]

Then saw I many a glow, living and conquering, make of us a center,
and of themselves a crown ; sweeter in voice than shining in
appearance.
Thus girt we sometimes see Latona's daughter, when the air is so
impregnated as to retain the thread that makes her zone.

In Canto X, lines 70–81, he describes their manifestation of
joy :

[30] *Paradiso*, IX, 31–33.
[31] *Paradiso*, X, 64–69.

In the court of heaven, whence I have returned, are many gems so
  clear and beauteous that from that realm they may not be withdrawn,
and the song of these lights was of such that he who doth not so wing
  himself that he may fly up there, must look for news thence from
  the dumb.
When, so singing, those burning suns had circled round us thrice,
  like stars neighboring the fixed poles,
they seemed as ladies, not from the dance released, but silent, listening
  till they catch the notes renewed.

With constant light, and ever-increasing melody the ascent
continues. To the double rainbow : [32]

As sweep o'er the thin mist two bows, parallel and like in color,
  when Juno maketh behest to her handmaiden,
the one without born from the one within—in fashion of the speech
  of that wandering nymph whom love consumed as the sun doth
  the vapors,—
making folk on earth foreknow, in virtue of the compact that God
  made with Noah, that the world shall never be drowned again ;
so of those sempiternal roses there revolved around us the two garlands,
  and so the outmost answered to the other :
Soon as the dance and high great festival,—alike of song and flashing
  light with light, gladsome and benign,—paused at one point and
  one desire.

In the fifth heaven (that of Mars) glows the glorious cross of
stars, recalling by its difference the vision of the Saxon Caedmon.

Canto XIV, 97–111

As, pricked out with less and greater lights, between the poles of the
  universe the Milky Way so gleameth white as to set very sages
  questioning,
so did those rays, star-decked, make in the depth of Mars[33] the venerable
  sign which crossing quadrant lines make in a circle.
Here my memory doth outrun my wit, for that cross so flashed forth
  Christ I may not find example worthy.

[32] *Paradiso*, XII, 10–24.
[33] i.e. not in the planet, but the heaven in which the planet moves.

But whoso taketh his cross and followeth Christ shall yet forgive
me what I leave unsaid, when he shall see Christ lighten in that
glow.

From horn to horn, from summit unto base, were moving lights that
sparkled mightily in meeting one another and in passing."

And the accompanying melody :

And as viol and harp tuned in harmony of many cords, make sweet
chiming to one by whom the notes are not apprehended,

so from the lights that there appeared to me was gathered on the cross
a strain that rapt me, albeit I followed not the hymn.

Line 133, " I vivi suggelli d' ogni bellezza " recalls Richard
St. Victor's luminous treatise, *The Benjamin Minor*.

Canto XV, 13–24

As through the tranquil and pure skies darteth, from time to time,
a sudden flame setting a-moving eyes that erst were steady,

seeming a star that changeth place, save that from where it kindleth
no star is lost, and that itself endureth but a little ;

such from the horn that stretcheth to the right unto that cross's foot,
darteth a star of the constellation that is there a-glow ;

nor did the gem depart from off its riband, but coursed along the
radial line, like fire burning behind alabaster.[34]

In Canto XVII, Cacciaguida, prophesying to Dante his
future misfortunes, utters the lines (58–60) since hackneyed :

Thou shalt make trial of how salt doth taste another's bread, and how
hard the path to descend and mount upon another's stair.

The word " scale " contains the barbed pun on Can Grande's
family name. But no one can take the quiet humor as ill-
natured, or read it apart from the context in praise of Bartolomeo
and Can Grande in lines 70–87 :

[34] Che parve foco retro ad alabastro.

148

Thy first refuge and first hostelry shall be the courtesy of the great
 Lombard, who on the ladder beareth the sacred bird,
for who shall cast so benign regard on thee that of doing and demanding,
 that shall be first betwixt you two, which betwixt others most
 doth lag.
With him thou shalt see the one who so at his birth was stamped by
 this strong star, that notable shall be his deeds.
Not yet have folk taken due note of him, because of his young age,
 for only nine years have these wheels rolled round him.
But ere the Gascon have deceived the lofty Henry, sparks of his virtue
 shall appear in carelessness of silver and of toils.
His deeds munificent shall yet be known so that concerning them his
 very foes shall not be able to keep silent tongues.

The *Paradiso* holds one by its pervading sense of beauty ;
even so, lines 79–80 of Canto XXIII stand out from the surrounding text.

As, by the light of a sun-ray coming through a broken cloud,
mine eyes have before seen a meadow of flowers covered with shadow,
so did I see more hosts of splendors, illumined from above by ardent
light, yet saw not the source of the effulgence.

It is beautiful because of the objective vision, and it is all the
more remarkable in having been written centuries before the
painters had taught men to note light and shade, and to watch
for such effects in nature.

In this same canto Dante anticipates Coleridge's most magical
definition of beauty—καλον *quasi* χαλουν—in lines 97–102 :

Whatever melody most sweetly soundeth on earth, and doth
most *draw the soul unto itself*, would seem a rent cloud's thundering,
compared to the sound of that lyre, whereby is crowned that sapphire
whereby the clearest heaven is ensapphired.

With what Homeric majesty, and what simplicity falls his
epithet for that sphere which whirls the largest, the *primum
mobile*, most volent of the concentric spheres,

   " Lo real manto "—" The royal mantle."

The simile[35] shows how well he had followed Arnaut Daniel :

As the spray which boweth its tip at the transit of the wind, and then of its own power doth raise it again ; so I while Beatrice was speaking.

It is no borrowing, but it is Arnaut's kind of beauty.

In Canto XXVIII we find what seems to me the finest of the explanatory passages ; it concerns the angelic hierarchies :

> And thou shouldst know that all have their delight
> In measure as their sight more deeply sinketh
> Into that truth where every mind grows still ;
> From this thou mayest see that being blessèd
> Buildeth itself upon the power of sight
> Not upon love which is there-consequent.
> Lo, merit hath its measure in that sight
> Which grace begetteth and the righteous will,
> And thus from grade to grade the progress goeth.

The vigor of sunlight in the *Paradiso* is unmatched in art, even by Blake's design, " When the morning stars sang together " ; being a quality of the whole it is hard to illustrate by fragments ; it is, however, reflected in the following lines :[36]

The second ternary which thus flowereth in this eternal spring, which nightly Aries despoileth not, unceasingly unwintereth ' Hosanna ' with three melodies, which sound in the three orders of joy wherewith it is triplex.

And in line 76 of Canto XXIX :

> Queste sustanzie, poichè fur gioconde
> della faccia di Dio.

Lines 142-146 of the same canto are untranslatable :

[35] *Paradiso*, XXVI, 85.
[36] *Paradiso*, XXVIII, 115-120.

Vedi l'eccelso omai, e la larghezza
dell' eterno valor, poscia che tanti
speculi fatti s' ha, in che si spezza,
uno manendo in sè, come davanti.

In Canto XXX begins the description of the ultimate heaven, the Empyrean of pure light. Fainting, restored, and again illumined, Dante continues :[37]

And I saw light in the form of a river, tawny with brightness, between two banks painted with miraculous spring-time.

From such a flood there issued living sparks, and dropped on every side into the flowers, like unto rubies which gold circumscribes.

Then, as if drunk with the odors, they re-plunged themselves[38] into the marvelous torrent, and as one entered another issued forth.

In lines 76–8 Beatrice says of the river :

The river and the topaz-gems which enter and go forth are shadowy prefaces of their truth.

Lines 109–129 describe the paradisal rose :

And as in water a hill-slope mirrors itself from its base, as if to see itself adorned, when it is richest in grasses and in flowers.

So mounting above the light, circle on circle, mirroring itself in more than a thousand thresholds all that (part) of us which hath won return up thither.

And if the lowest step gathereth in itself such great light, what is the largess of that rose in its extremest petals ?

My sight fainted not in the breadth and height, but understood the ' How much ' and the ' What sort ' of that joy.

There neither ' Near ' nor ' Far ' doth add nor take away, for where God governeth without medium, natural law pertaineth not.

Into the yellow of the sempiternal rose, which dilates and outstretches, and sendeth up the odor of praise unto the Sun that ever giveth forth Spring,

Beatrice drew me up, I being as one who would keep silence and

[37] *Paradiso*, XXX, 61–69.
[38] riprofondavan sè.

yet speak, and she said to me : ' Behold, how great is the convent
of the white stoles ! '

Of the angels and the rose :[39]

As a swarm of bees that now inflowereth itself, and now returneth
to where its labor is made honey,
they descended into the great flower that is adorned with so many
petals, and thence reascended to that place where their love sojourneth
ever.
Faces had they of living brightness, and golden wings, and the rest
of them of whiteness that no snow ever attaineth.

To Beatrice, when she has resumed her place in the rose, he
says :

O lady, in whom is the might of my hope, who hast for my salvation suffered thyself to leave in Hell thy foot-prints ;
For all the things which I have seen, I recognize the grace and the
might of thy power and of thy kindness.
From slavery hast thou drawn me into liberty, by all the roads
and by all the modes wherein thou hast had power of action.

These nine lines, taken apart from the context are, I suppose,
the noblest love lyric in the world, unless we shall bring the
" Magnificat " itself into the comparison.
Of Mary :[40]

> Vidi quivi ai lor giochi ed ai lor canti
> ridere una bellezza, che letizia
> era negli occhi a tutti gli altri santi.

Of the final manifestation he writes :[41]

Thence was the vision mightier than our speech, which at such
vision faileth, and memory faileth concerning such a ' passing beyond.'
As one who dreaming seeth, and after the dream, the passion impressed
remaineth, while naught else cometh back upon the mind ;

[39] *Paradiso*, XXXI, 7–18.
[40] *Paradiso*, XXI, 133–135.
[41] *Paradiso*, XXXIII, 55–66.

Such was I, so that nearly all my vision ceaseth, but the sweet which was born thereof still distilleth itself within the heart.

Thus doth the snow before the sun unstamp itself, thus in the light leaves upon the wind was lost the Sybil's saying.

In lines 85–89 of the final canto :

In its profound I saw contain itself, bound by love into one volume, that which is read throughout the universe ; substance and accidents and their customs, in such wise that that which I speak is a simple light.

And then the conclusion :

O light eternal, that dost dwell only in thyself, alone dost comprehend thyself, and self-comprehended, self-comprehending, dost love and send forth gladness !

That circling, which so conceived appeared in thee as a reflected light, beheld awhile by my eyes, within itself, of its own color, appeared to me painted in our image, wherefore my sight was all committed to it.

As is the geometer who sets himself to square the circle, and does not find, by thinking, that principle whence he lacketh, such was I at this new sight ; I would have wished to see how the image conveneth to the circle, and how it is contained ; but for this my wings were unfitted, save that my mind was smitten by an effulgence, wherein its will came to it.

Power I lack for this high fantasy, but already my desire and the will were turned, as a wheel which is balanced perfectly and moveth, by love that moves the sun and all the stars.[42]

Surely for the great poem that ends herewith our befitting praise were silence.

The *Divina Commedia* must not be considered as an epic ; to compare it with epic poems is usually unprofitable. It is in a sense lyric, the tremendous lyric of the subjective Dante ; but the soundest classification of the poem is Dante's own, " as a comedy which differs from tragedy in its content,"[43] for " tragedy begins admirably and tranquilly," and the end

[42] L'amor che move il sole e l' altre stelle.
[43] *Epistle to Can Grande.*

is terrible, " whereas comedy introduces some harsh complication, but brings the matter to a prosperous end." The *Commedia* is, in fact, a great mystery play, or better, a cycle of mystery plays.

In the passages quoted I have in no way attempted to summarize the *Commedia* ; it is itself an epitome. I have tried to illustrate some, not all, of the qualities of its beauty, but Dante in English is Marsyas unsheathed.

Any sincere criticism of the highest poetry must resolve itself into a sort of profession of faith. The critic must begin with a " credo," and his opinion will be received in part for the intelligence he may seem to possess, and in part for his earnestness. Certain of Dante's supremacies are comprehensible only to such as know Italian and have themselves attained a certain proficiency in the poetic art. An *ipse dixit* is not necessarily valueless. The penalty for remaining a layman is that one must at times accept a specialist's opinion. No one ever took the trouble to become a specialist for the bare pleasure of ramming his *ipse dixit* down the general throat.

There are two kinds of beautiful painting one may perhaps illustrate by the works of Burne-Jones and Whistler ; one looks at the first kind of painting and is immediately delighted by its beauty ; the second kind of painting, when first seen, puzzles one, but on leaving it, and going from the gallery one finds new beauty in natural things—a Thames fog, to use the hackneyed example. Thus, there are works of art which are beautiful objects and works of art which are keys or passwords admitting one to a deeper knowledge, to a finer perception of beauty ; Dante's work is of the second sort.

Presumably critical analysis must precede in part by comparison ; Wordsworth is, we may say, the orthodox sign for comprehension of nature, yet where has Wordsworth written lines more instinct with " nature-feeling " than those in the twenty-eight of the *Purgatorio*.

> l' aqua diss' io, e il suon della foresta
> impugnan dentro a me novella fede.
> The water, quoth I, and the woodland murmuring
> drive in new faith upon my soul.

So one is tempted to translate it for the sake of the rhythm, but Dante has escaped the metaphysical term, and describes the actual sensation with more intensity. His words are : " in-drive new faith within to me."

Wordsworth and the Uncouth American share the palm for modern " pantheism," or some such thing ; but weigh their words with the opening lines of the *Paradiso* :

> La gloria di colui che tutto move
> Per l' universo penetra e risplende
> In una parte più, e meno altrove.

> The glory of him who moveth all
> Penetrates and is resplendent through the all
> In one part more and in another less.

The disciples of Whitman cry out concerning the " cosmic sense," but Whitman, with all his catalogues and flounderings, has never so perfectly expressed the perception of cosmic consciousness as does Dante in the canto just quoted :[44]

> Qual si fe' Glauco nel gustar dell' erba
> Che il fe' consorto in mar degli altri dei.

> As Glaucus, tasting of the grass which made him
> sea-fellow of the other gods.

Take it as simple prose expression, forget that it is told with matchless sound, discount the suggestion of the parallel beauty in the older myth, and it is still more convincing than Whitman.

Shelley, I believe, ranks highest as the English " transcendental " poet, whatever that may mean. Shelley is honest in

[44] *Paradiso*, I, 68–9.

his endeavor to translate a part of Dante's message into the more northern tongue. He is, in sort, a faint echo of the *Paradiso*, very much as Rossetti is, at his best, an echo of the shorter Tuscan poetry. I doubt if Shelley ever thought of concealing the source of much of this beauty, which he made his own by appreciation. Certainly few men have honored Dante more than did Shelley. His finest poem, *The Ode to the West Wind*, bears witness to his impressions of the earlier canti ; thus to the host under the whirling ensign in Canto III of the *Inferno*, and especially to lines 112–115 :

> Come d' autunno si levan le foglie
> L' uno appreso dell' altra infin che il ramo
> Vede alla terra tutte le sue spoglie.

> As leaves of autumn fall one after one
> Till the branch seeth all its spoils upon
> The ground. . . .

The full passage from which this is taken foreshadows Shelley's " pestilence-stricken multitudes." In the fifth canto " shadows borne upon the aforesaid strife,"[45] and the rest, with the movement of the wind, is pregnant with suggestions for the splendid English ode. I detract nothing from Shelley's glory, for of the tens of thousands who have read these canti, only one has written such an ode.

This is not an isolated or a chance incident ; the best of Shelley is filled with memories of Dante.

The comparison of Dante and Milton is at best a stupid convention. Shelley resembles Dante afar off, and in a certain effect of clear light which both produce.

Milton resembles Dante in nothing ; judging superficially, one might say that they both wrote long poems which mention God and the angels, but their gods and their angels are as different as their styles and abilities. Dante's god is ineffable divinity.

[45] Ombre portate della detta briga.

Milton's god is a fussy old man with a hobby. Dante is meta-physical, where Milton is merely sectarian. *Paradise Lost* is conventional melodrama, and later critics have decided that the Devil is intended for the hero, which interpretation leaves the whole without significance. Dante's Satan is undeniably and indelibly evil. He is not "Free Will" but stupid malignity. Milton has no grasp of the superhuman. Milton's angels are men of enlarged power, plus wings. Dante's angels surpass human nature, and differ from it. They move in their high courses inexplicable.

> *ma fe sembiante*
> *d' uomo, cui altra cura stringa.*
> Appeared as a man whom other care incites.[46]

Milton, moreover, shows a complete ignorance of the things of the spirit. Any attempt to compare the two poets as equals is bathos, and it is, incidentally, unfair to Milton, because it makes one forget all his laudable qualities.

Shakespear alone of the English poets endures sustained comparison with the Florentine. Here are we with the masters ; of neither can we say, " He is the greater " ; of each we must say, " He is unexcelled."

It is idle to ask what Dante would have made of writing stage plays, or what Shakespear would have done with a " Paradise."

There is almost an exact three centuries between their dates of birth [Dante was born in 1265 ; Shakespear in 1564]. America had been discovered, printing, the Reformation, the Renaissance were new forces at work. Much change had swept over the world ; but art and humanity, remaining ever the same, gave us basis for comparison.

Dante would seem to have the greater imaginative " vision," the greater ability to see the marvellous scenery through which

[46] *Inferno,* IX, 101.

his action passes ; but Shakespear's vision is never deficient, though his expression of it be confined to a few lines of suggestion and the prose of the stage directions.

Shakespear would seem to have greater power in depicting various humanity, and to be more observant of its foibles ; but recalling Dante's comparisons to the gamester leaving the play, to the peasant at the time of hoar-frost, to the folk passing in the shadow of evening, one wonders if he would have been less apt at fitting them with speeches. His dialogue is comparatively symbolic, it serves a purpose similar to that of the speeches in Plato, yet both he and Plato convey the impression of individuals speaking.

If the language of Shakespear is more beautifully suggestive, that of Dante is more beautifully definite ; both men are masters of the whole art. Shakespear is perhaps more brilliant in his use of epithets of proper quality ; thus I doubt if there be in Dante, or in all literature, any epithet so masterfully-placed as is Shakespear's in the speech of the Queen-mother to Hamlet where she says " And with the incorporal air do hold discourse," suggesting both the common void of the air which she sees and the ghostly form at which Hamlet stands aghast ; on the other hand, Dante is, perhaps, more apt in " comparison."

" The apt use of metaphor, arising, as it does, from a swift perception of relations, is the hall-mark of genius " : thus says Aristotle. I use the term " comparison " to include metaphor, simile (which is a more leisurely expression of a kindred variety of thought), and the " language beyond metaphor," that is, the more compressed or elliptical expression of metaphorical perception, such as antithesis suggested or implied in verbs and adjectives ; for we find adjectives of two sorts, thus, adjectives of pure quality, as : white, cold, ancient ; and adjectives which are comparative, as : lordly. Epithets may also be distinguished as epithets of primary and secondary apparition. By epithets of primary apparition I mean those which describe what is actually presented to the sense or vision. Thus in " selva oscura," ("shadowy wood"); epithets of secondary apparition or after-thought are such as in "*sage* Hippotades" or "*forbidden* tree." Epithets of primary apparition give vividness to description and stimulate conviction in the actual vision of the poet. There are likewise clauses and phrases of "primary apparition," Thus, in Canto X of the *Inferno*, where Cavalcante di Cavalcanti's head appears above the edge of the tomb, "I believe he had risen on his knees,"[47] has no beauty in itself, but adds greatly to the verisimilitude.

There are also epithets of "emotional apparition," transensu-ous, suggestive as in Yeats' line, "Under a bitter *black* wind that blows from the left hand." Dante's coloring and qualities of the infernal air, although they are definitely symbolical and not indefinitely suggestive, foreshadow this sort of epithet. The modern symbolism is more vague, it is sometimes allegory in three dimensions instead of two, sometimes merely atmospheric suggestion.

It is in the swift forms of comparison, however, that Dante sets much of his beauty. Thus: "dove il sol tace," ("where the sun is silent,") or, "l'aura morta," ("the dead air."). In this last the comparison fades imperceptibly into emotional suggestion.

His vividness depends much on his comparison by simile to particular phenomena; this we have already noted in the chapter on Arnaut Daniel; thus Dante, following the Provençal, says, not "where a river pools itself," but "As at Arles, where the Rhone pools itself."[48] Or when he is describing not a scene but a feeling, he makes such comparison as in the matchless simile to Glaucus, already quoted.

Dante's temperament is austere, patrician; Shakespear, as nature, combines refinement with profusion; it is as natural to compare Dante to a cathedral as it is to compare Shakespear to a forest; yet Shakespear is not more enamored of out-of-door

[47] Credo che s'era in ginocchie levata.
[48] Si come ad Arli, ove il Rodano stagna.

beauty than is Dante. Their lands make them familiar with a
different sort of out-of-doors. Shakespear shows his affection
for this beauty as he knows it in—

> —the morn, in russet mantle clad,
> Walks o'er the dew of yon high eastward hill ;

and Dante, when the hoar frost

> paints her white sister's image on the ground.

It is part of Dante's aristocracy that he conceded nothing to
the world, or to opinion—like Farinata, he met his reverses
" as if he held Hell in great disdain "[49] ; Shakespear concedes,
succeeds, and repents in one swift, bitter line : " I have made
myself a motley to the view."

Shakespear comes nearer to most men, partly from his habit
of speaking from inside his characters instead of conversing with
them. He seems more human, but only when we forget the
intimate confession of the *Vita Nuova* or such lines of the
Commedia as

> col quale il fantolin corre alla mamma
> quand' ha paura o quando egli è aflitto.

> as the little child runs to its mother when it
> has fear, or when it is hurt.

Dante has the advantage in points of pure sound ; his onomatopoeia is not a mere trick of imitating natural noises, but is a
mastery in fitting the inarticulate sound of a passage to the
mood or to the quality of voice which expresses that mood or
passion which the passage describes or expresses. Shakespear
has a language less apt for this work in pure sound, but he
understands the motion of words, or, if the term be permitted,
the overtones and undertones of rhythm, and he uses them with
a mastery which no one but Burns has come reasonably near
to approaching. Other English poets master this part of the

[49] " Si come avesse l' inferno in gran dispetto."

art occasionally, or as if by accident ; there is a fine example in a passage of Sturge Moore's *Defeat of the Amazons*, where the spirit of his faun leaps and scurries, with the words beginning : " Ahi ! ahi ! ahi ! Laomedon."

This government of speed is a very different thing from the surge and sway of the epic music where the smoother rhythm is so merged with the sound quality as to be almost inextricable. The two things compare almost as the rhythm of a drum compares to the rhythm (not the sound) of the violin or organ. Thus, the " surge and sway " are wonderful in Swinburne's first chorus in the *Atalanta* ; while the other quality of word motion is most easily distinguished in, though by no means confined to, such poems as Burns' *Birks o' Aberfeldy*, where the actual sound-quality of the words contributes little or nothing to the effect, which is dependent solely on the arrangment of quantities (*i.e.* the lengths of syllables) and accent. It is not, as it might first seem, a question of vowel music as opposed to consonant music.

For such as are interested in the question of sources, it may be well to write, once for all, that there is nothing particularly new in describing the journey of a living man through Hell, or even of his translation into Paradise ; Arda Virap, in the Zoroastrian legend, was sent as ambassador, in the most accredited fashion ; with full credentials he ascended into Paradise, and saw the pains of Hell shortly afterwards. The description of such journeys may be regarded as a confirmed literary habit of the race.

The question of Shakespear's debt to Dante and the Tuscan poets is not of vital importance. It is true that a line of Shakespear is often a finer expression of a Dantescan thought than any mere translator of Dante has hit upon, but nothing is more natural than that the two greatest poets of Christendom, holding up their mirrors to nature, should occasionally reflect the same detail. It is true that Shakespear's lines :

> What is your substance, whereof are you made,
> That millions of strange shadows on you tend ?

seem like a marriage of words from Guido Orlandi's sonnet to Guido Cavalcanti, and from one of Cavalcanti's sonnets which I have quoted.

Mascetta Caracci has written a thesis on " Shakespear e i classici Italiani," multiplying instances.

Early Tuscan sonnets are often very " Elizabethan," and the Spanish imitations of the Tuscans are often more so. Great poets seldom make bricks without straw ; they pile up all the excellences they can beg, borrow, or steal from their predecessors and contemporaries, and then set their own inimitable light atop of the mountain. It seems unlikely that the author of *The Sonnets* should have been ignorant of the finest sonnets in the world, or that a man of Shakespear's literary discernment should have read Bandello and not the Italian masters. Shakespear knew of Gower, and Gower and Chaucer knew of Dante. As Shakespear wrote the finest poetry in English, it matters not one jot whether or no he plundered the Italian lyrists in his general sack of available literature.

That Shakespear, as Dante, is the conscious master of his art is most patent from the manner in which he plays with his art in the sonnets, teasing, experimenting, developing that technique which he so marvellously uses and so cunningly conceals in the later plays. To talk about "wood-notes wild" is sheer imbecility.

Did Shakespear know his Tuscan poetry directly or through some medium, through Petrarch, or through some Italianized Englishman ? Why did he not write a play on Francesca da Rimini ? There are a number of subjects for amusing speculation ; theories will be built from straws floating in the wind ; thus Francis Meres, when in 1598 he writes of Shakespear's " fine-filed phrase," may or may not have some half memory of Dante's " amorosa lima," the " loving file " that had " polished his speech."

Our knowledge of Dante and of Shakespear interacts ; intimate acquaintance with either breeds that discrimination which makes us more keenly appreciate the other.

One might indefinitely continue the praise of Dante's excellence of technique and his splendors of detail ; but beneath these individual and separate delights is the great sub-surge of his truth and his sincerity : his work is that sort of art which is a key to the deeper understanding of nature and the beauty of the world and of the spirit. From his descriptions of the aspects of nature I have already quoted the passage of the sunlight and the cloud shadows ; for the praise of that part of his worth which is fibre rather than surface, my mind is not yet ripe, nor is my pen skilled.

Let these speak for me ; first, John Boccaccio, as translated by Rossetti :

> *To one who censured his Public Exposition of Dante*
> If Dante mourns, there wheresoe'er he be,
> That such high fancies of a soul so proud
> Should be laid open to the vulgar crowd,
> (As, touching my discourse, I'm told by thee,)
> This were my grievous pain ; and certainly
> My proper blame should not be disavow'd ;
> Though hereof somewhat, I declare aloud,
> Were due to others, not alone to me.
> False hopes, true poverty, and therewithal
> The blinded judgment of a host of friends,
> And their entreaties, made that I did thus.
> But of all this there is no gain at all
> Unto the thankless souls with whose base ends
> Nothing agrees that's great or generous.

and :

> *Inscription for a Portrait of Dante*
> Dante Alighieri, a dark oracle
> Of wisdom and of art I am, whose mind
> Has to my country such great gifts assign'd
> That men account my powers a miracle.
> My lofty fancy pass'd as low as Hell,
> As high as Heaven, secure and unconfined ;
> And in my noble book doth every kind
> Of earthly lore and heavenly doctrine dwell.
> Renowned Florence was my mother,—nay,

Stepmother with me her piteous son,
Through sin of cursed slander's tongue and tooth.
Ravenna shelter'd me so cast away;
My body is with her,—my soul with One
For whom no envy can make dim the truth.

or Michael Agnolo, as translated by J. A. Symonds:

On Dante Alighieri

I

From heaven his spirit came, and robed in clay
  The realms of justice and of mercy trod,
  Then rose a living man to gaze on God,
  That he might make the truth as clear as day.
For that pure star that brightened with his ray
  The undeserving nest where I was born,
  The whole wide world would be a prize to scorn;
  None but his Maker can due guerdon pay.
I speak of Dante, whose high work remains
  Unknown, unhonored by that thankless brood,
  Who only to just men deny their wage.
Were I but he! Born for like lingering pains,
  Against his exile coupled with his good
  I'd gladly change the world's best heritage!

II

No tongue can tell of him what should be told,
  For on blind eyes his splendor shines too strong;
  'Twere easier to blame those who wrought him wrong
  Than sound his least praise with a mouth of gold.
He to explore the place of pain was bold,
  Then soared to God, to reach our souls by song;
  The gates heaven oped to bear his feet along,
  Against his just desire his country rolled.
Thankless I call her, and to her own pain
  The nurse of fell mischance; for sign take this,
  That ever to the best she deals more scorn:
Among a thousand proofs let one remain;
  Though ne'er was fortune more unjust than his,
  His equal or his better ne'er was born.

TABLE OF DATES

Arnaut Daniel	circa	1180–1200
Guido Guincelli	born	1220
Dante		1265–1321
Petrarch		1304–1374
Boccaccio		1313–1375
Chaucer		1340–1400
Gower	died	1408
Villon		1431–after 1465
Michael Agnolo		1475–1564
Camoens	born	1524
Lope de Vega		1562–1635
Shakespear		1564–1616

VIII

The century between Dante and Villon brought into the poetry of northern Europe no element which was distinctly new. The plant of the Renaissance was growing, a plant which some say begins in Dante ; but Dante, I think, anticipates the Renaissance only as one year's harvest foreshadows the next year's Spring. He is the culmination of one age rather than the beginning of the next ; he is like certain buildings in Verona, which display the splendor of the Middle Ages, untouched by any influence of the classic revival.

In architecture, mediæval work means line ; line, composition and design : Renaissance work means mass. The Gothic architect envied the spider his cobweb. The Renaissance architect sought to rival the mountain. They raised successively the temple of the spirit and the temple of the body. The analogy in literature is naturally inexact ; Dante, however, sought to hang his song from the absolute, the center and source of light ; art since Dante has for the most part built from the ground.

General formulas of art criticism serve at best to suggest a train of thought, or a manner of examining the individual works of a period. Such formulas are not figures circumscribing the works of art, but points from which to compute their dimensions.

The Renaissance is not a time, but a temperament. Petrarch and Boccaccio have it. To the art of poetry they bring nothing distinctive : Petrarch refines but deenergizes.[1] In England,

---

[1] 1929 : No, he doesn't even refine, he oils and smooths over the idiom. As far as any question of actual fineness of emotion or cadence or perception he is miles behind Ventadorn or Arnaut Daniel. Petrarch systematizes a certain ease of verbal expression in Italian. An excellent author for an Italian law student seeking to improve his " delivery."

Gower had written pleasantly, and " Romance," the romance of the longer narratives, had come to full fruit in Chaucer. Where Dante is a crystallization of many mediæval elements, his own intensity the cause of their cohesion, Chaucer comes as through a more gradual, gentler process, like some ultimate richer blossom on that bough which brought forth Beroul, Thomas, Marie, Crestien, Wace, and Gower. He is part, some will say, of the humanistic revolt. There was no abrupt humanistic revolt. Boccaccio and the rest but carry on a paganism which had never expired.

After all these fine gentlemen, guardians of the Arthurian Graal, prophets of Rome's rejuvenation, and the rest, had been laid in their graves, there walked the gutters of Paris one François Montcorbier, poet and gaol-bird, with no care whatever for the flowery traditions of mediæval art, and no anxiety to revive the massive rhetoric of the Romans. Yet whatever seeds of the Renaissance there may have been in Dante, there were seeds or signs of a far more modern outbreak in the rhymes of this Montcorbier, *alias* Villon.

The minstrelsy of Provence is as the heart of Sir Blancatz, and the later lords of song, in England and in Tuscany, have eaten well of it. From Provence the Tuscans have learned pattern ; the Elizabethans a certain lyric quality ; Villon carries on another Provençal tradition, that of unvarnished, intimate speech. I do not imply that Villon is directly influenced by Provence, but that some of his notes and fashions had been already sounded in Provence. Thus the tone of a tenzone of Arnaut Daniel's, not quoted in Chapter II, suggests the tone of some of Villon's verses ; even as the form of the Provençal canzon had suggested the form of the north French ballade.

Villon's abuse finds precedent in the lower type of sirvente, with this distinction, that Villon at times says of himself what the Provençals said only of one another. For precedent of Villon's outspokenness one need not seek so far as Provence. The French mystery plays are not written in veiled words.

To witness, this passage from a Crucifixion play, when an angel says to God the Father :

> Père éternal, vous avez tort
> E ben devetz avoir vergogne.
> Vostre fils bien amis est mort
> E vous dormez comme un ivrogne.
>
> Father eternal, you are wrong
> And well should be shamed,
> Your well beloved son is dead
> And you sleep like a drunk.

Villon's art exists because of Villon. There is in him no pretence of the man sacrificed to his labor. One may define him unsatisfactorily by a negative comparison with certain other poets, thus : where Dante has boldness of imagination, Villon has the stubborn persistency of one whose gaze cannot be deflected from the actual fact before him : what he sees, he writes. Dante is in some ways one of the most personal of poets ; he holds up the mirror to nature, but he is himself that mirror.

Villon never forgets his fascinating, revolting self. If, however, he sings the song of himself he is, thank God, free from that horrible air of rectitude with which Whitman rejoices in being Whitman. Villon's song is selfish through self-absorption ; he does not, as Whitman, pretend to be conferring a philantropic benefit on the race by recording his own self-complacency. Human misery is more stable than human dignity ; there is more intensity in the passion of cold, remorse, hunger, and the fetid damp of the mediæval dungeon than in eating water melons. Villon is a voice of suffering, of mockery, of irrevocable fact ; Whitman is the voice of one who saith :

> Lo, behold, I eat water-melons. When I eat water-melons the
> world eats water-melons through me.
> When the world eats water-melons, I partake of the world's
> water-melons.

The bugs,
The worms.
The negroes, etc.,
Eat water-melons ; All nature eats water-melons.
Those eidolons and particles of the Cosmos
Which do not now partake of water-melons
Will at some future time partake of water-melons.
Praised be Allah or Ramanathanath Khrishna !

They call it optimism, and breadth of vision. There is, in the poetry of François Villon, neither optimism nor breadth of vision.

Villon is shameless. Whitman, having decided that it is disgraceful to be ashamed, rejoices in having attained nudity.

Goethe, when the joys of taxidermy sufficed not to maintain his self-respect, was wont to rejoice that there was something noble and divine in being *Künstler*. The artist is an artist and therefore admirable, or noble, or something of that sort. If Villon ever discovered this pleasant mode of self-deception, he had sense enough not to say so in rhyme. In fact, Villon himself may be considered sufficient evidence seriously to damage this artist-consoling theory.

Villon holds his unique place in literature because he is the only poet without illusions. There are *désillusionnés*, but they are different ; Villon set forth without the fragile cargo. Villon never lies to himself ; he does not know much, but what he knows he knows : man is an animal, certain things he can feel ; there is much misery, man has a soul about which he knows little or nothing. Helen, Heloise and Joan are dead, and you will gather last year's snows before you find them.

Thus the *Ballade of Dead Ladies* :

> Tell me now in what hidden way is
>   Lady Flora, the lovely Roman,
> Where is Hipparchia and where is Thaïs,
>   Neither of them the fairer woman,
> Where is Echo, beheld of no man,
>   Only heard on river and mere,
> She whose beauty was more than human ?
>   But where are the snows of yester-year !

THE SPIRIT OF ROMANCE

And where are Beatris, Alys, Hermengarde, and

> That good Joan whom Englishmen
> At Rouen doomed, and burned her there !
> Mother of God, where are they, where ?
> But where are the snows of yester-year ![2]

Of his further knowledge,

> I know a horse from a mule,
> And Beatrix from Bellet,
> I know the heresy of the Bohemians,
> I know son, valet and man.
> I know all things save myself alone.

Or in the *Grand Testament,*

> Je suis pecheur, je le scay bien
> Pourtant Dieu ne veut pas ma mort.

> I am a sinner, I know it well,
> However, God does not wish my death.

Or in the ballade quoted :

> Je cognois mort qui nous consomme,
> Je cognois tout fors que moi mesme.

> And I know Death that downs us all,
> I know all things save myself alone.

It is not Villon's art, but his substance, that pertains. Where Dante is the supreme artist, Villon is incurious ; he accepts the forms of verse as unquestioningly as he accepts the dogma and opinion of his time. If Dante reaches out of his time, and by rising above it escapes many of its limitations, Villon in some way speaks below the voice of his age's convention, and thereby outlasts it. He is utterly mediæval, yet his poems mark the

[2] Compare " Les Coplas " of Villon's Spanish contemporary Gomez Manrique.

end of mediæval literature. Dante strives constantly for a nobler state on earth. His aspiration separates him from his time, and the ordinary reader from his work. The might of his imagination baffles the many. Villon is destitute of imagination ; he is almost destitute of art ; he has no literary ambition, no consciousness of the fame hovering over him ; he has some slight vanity in impressing his immediate audience, more in reaching the ear of Louis XI by a ballade—this last under pressure of grave necessity.

Much of both the *Lesser* and the *Greater Testaments* is in no sense poetry ; the wit is of the crudest ; thief, murderer,[3] pander, bully to a whore, he is honored for a few score pages of unimaginative sincerity ; he sings of things as they are. He dares to show himself. His depravity is not a pose cultivated for literary effect. He never makes the fatal mistake of glorifying his sin, of rejoicing in it, or of pretending to despise its opposite. His " Ne voient pan qu'aux fenestres," is no weak moralizing on the spiritual benefits of fasting.

The poignant stanzas in which this line occurs, are comparable only to Lamb's graver and more plaintive, " I have had playmates, I have had companions."

Grand Testament

XXIX

Where are the gracious gallants
That I beheld in times gone by.
Singing so well, so well speaking,
So pleasant in act and in word.
Some are dead and stiffened,
Of them there is nothing more now.
May they have rest, but in Paradise,
And God save the rest of them.

---

[3] This may be a little severe. Murder was not his habit ; we may, however, believe that he had killed his man.

XXX

And some are become
God's mercy ! great lords and masters,
And others beg all naked
And see no bread, save in the windows ;
Others have gone into the cloisters
Of Celestin and of Chartreuse,
Shod and hosed like fishers of oysters.
Behold the divers state among them all.

Villon paints himself, as Rembrandt painted his own hideous
face ; his few poems drive themselves into one in a way un-
approached by the delicate art of a Daniel or a Baudelaire.
Villon makes excuses neither for God nor for himself ; he does
not rail at providence because its laws are not adjusted to punish
all weaknesses except his own. There is, perhaps, no more
poignant regret than that stanza in *Le Grand Testament*,

Je plaings le temps de ma jeunesse.

I mourn the time of my youth,
When I made merry more than another,
Until the coming in of old age,
Which has sealed me its departure.
It is not gone on foot,
Nor on horseback ; alas ! and how then ?
Suddenly it has flown away,
And has left me nothing worth.[4]

XXIII

Gone it is, and I remain
Poor of sense and of savoir,
Sad, shattered, and more black than ripe
Sans coin or rent or anything mine own.

He recognizes the irrevocable, he blames no one but himself,
he never wastes time in self-reproaches, recognizing himself as
the result of irrevocable causes.

[4] Et ne m'a laissé quelque don.

Necessitè faict gens mesprendre
E faim saillir le loup des boys.

Necessity makes men run wry,
And hunger drives the wolf from wood.

He has the learning of the schools, or at least such smattering of it as would be expected from a brilliant, desultory auditor, but his wisdom is the wisdom of the gutter. The dramatic imagination is beyond him, yet having lived himself, he has no need to imagine what life is. His poems are gaunt as the *Poemà del Cid* is gaunt; they treat of actualities, they are untainted with fancy ; in the *Cid* death is death, war is war. In Villon filth is filth, crime is crime ; neither crime nor filth is gilded. They are not considered as strange delights and forbidden luxuries, accessible only to adventurous spirits. Passion he knows, and satiety he knows, and never does he forget their relation.

He scarcely ever takes the trouble to write anything he does not actually feel. When he does, as in the prayer made for his mother, the lament for Master Ythier's lost mistress, or the ballade for a young bridegroom, it is at the request of a particular person ; and the gaunt method in which he expresses his own feelings does not desert him. Even here the expression is that of such simple, general emotion that the verses can hardly be regarded as dramatic ; one almost imagines Villon asking Ythier or the bridegroom what they want written, and then rhyming it for them.

Thus this lay, or rather rondeau, which he bequeaths to Master Ythier who has lost his mistress :

Death, 'gainst thine harshness I appeal
That hath torn my leman from me,
Thou goest not yet contentedly
Though of sorrow of thee none doth me heal.
No power or might did she e'er wield,
In life what harm e'er did she thee
      Ah, Death !

Two we ! that with one heart did feel,
If she is dead, how then, dividedly
Shall I live on, sans life in me.
Save as do statues 'neath thy seal
    Thou Death !

(" Par coeur " in the last line of the original, has no equivalent in modern French or in English ; to dine " par coeur," by heart, is to dine on nothing.)

The same tendencies are apparent in the following ballade, that which Villon made at the request of his mother, " to be prayed to our lady." I give here stanzas I and III from Rossetti's translation.

I

Lady of Heaven and Earth, and therewithal
Crowned empress of the nether clefts of Hell,—
I, thy poor Christian, on thy name do call,
Commending me to thee, with thee to dwell,
Albeit in nought I be commendable.
But all mine undeserving may not mar
Such mercies as thy sovereign mercies are ;
Without the which (as true words testify)
No soul can reach thy Heaven so fair and far,
Even in this faith I choose to live and die.

III

A pitiful poor woman, shrunk and old,
I am, and nothing learned in letter-lore,
Within my parish-cloister I behold
A painted Heaven where harps and lutes adore,
And eke an Hell whose damned folk seethe full sore :
One bringeth fear, the other joy to me.
That joy, great goddess, make thou mine to be,—
Thou of whom all must ask it even as I ;
And that which faith desires, that let it see,
For in this faith I choose to live and die.

Another interesting translation of this poem is to be found

among the poems of the late J. M. Synge. For the ballade for
the bridegroom I refer to Payne or Swinburne.

Villon is, if you will, dramatic in his *Regrets of the Belle
Heaulmière*, but his own life was so nearly that of his wasted
armouress, that his voice is at one with hers. Indeed his own
" Je plains le temps de ma jeunesse " might almost be part of
this ballade.   Here are stanzas 1, 5 and 10 of Swinburne's
translation.

I

Meseemeth I heard cry and groan
That sweet who was the armourer's maid ;
For her young years she made sore moan,
And right upon this wise she said ;
' Ah fierce old age with foul bald head
To spoil fair things thou art over fain ;
Who holdeth me ? Who ? Would God I were dead !
Would God I were well dead and slain !

V

And he died thirty years agone.
I am old now, no sweet thing to see ;
By God, though when I think thereon,
And of that good glad time, woe's me,
And stare upon my changèd body
Stark naked, that has been so sweet,
Lean, wizen, like a small dry tree,
I am nigh mad with the pain of it.

X

So we make moan for the old sweet days,
Poor old light women, two or three
Squatting above the straw-fire's blaze,
The bosom crushed against the knee,
Like fagots on a heap we be,
Round fires soon lit, soon quenched and done,
And we were once so sweet, even we !
Thus fareth many and many an one.'

This ballade is followed in the *Testament* by the ballade of " La Belle Heaulmière aux filles de joie."

> Car vieilles n'ont ne cours ne estre
> Ne que monnoye qu'on descrie,

> For old they have not course nor status
> More than hath money that's turned in,

is the tune of it.

In *La Grosse Margot* from " ce bourdel ou tenons nostre estat," Villon casts out the dregs of his shame.

Many have attempted to follow Villon, mistaking a pose for his reality. These experimenters, searchers for sensation, have, I think, proved that the " taverns and the whores " are no more capable of producing poetry than are philosophy, culture, art, philology, noble character, conscientious effort, or any other panacea. If persistent effort and a desire to leave the world a beautiful heritage, were greatly availing, Ronsard, who is still under-rated, and Petrarch, who is not, would be among the highest masters. Villon's greatness is that he unconsciously proclaims man's divine right to be himself, the only one of the so-called " rights of man " which is not an artificial product. Villon is no theorist, he is an objective fact. He makes no apology—herein lies his strength ; Burns is weaker, because he is in harmony with doctrines that have been preached, and his ideas of equality are derivative. Villon never wrote anything so didactic in spirit as the " man's a man for a' that." He is scarcely affected by the thought of his time, because he scarcely thinks ; speculation, at any rate, is far from him. But I may be wrong here. If Villon speculates, the end of his speculation is Omar's age-old ending : " Came out by the same door wherein I went." At any rate, Villon's actions are the result of his passions and his weaknesses. Nothing is " sicklied o'er with the pale cast of thought."

As a type of debauchee he is eternal. He has sunk to the

gutter, knowing life a little above it ; thus he is able to realize
his condition, to see it objectively, instead of insensibly taking it
for granted.

Dante lives in his mind ; to him two blending thoughts
give a music perceptible as two blending notes of a lute. He is
in the real sense an idealist. He sings of true pleasures ; he sings
as exactly as Villon ; they are admirably in agreement : Dante
to the effect that there are supernormal pleasures, enjoyable
by man through the mind ; Villon to the effect that the lower
pleasures lead to no satisfaction, " e ne m' a laissé quelque don."
" Thenceforward was my vision mightier than the discourse,"
writes the Italian ; and Dante had gone living through Hell,
in no visionary sense. Villon lacked energy to clamber out.
Dante had gone on, fainting, aided, erect in his own strength ;
had gone on to sing of things more difficult. Villon's poetry
seems, when one comes directly from the *Paradiso*, more vital,
more vivid ; but if Dante restrains himself, putting the laments
in the mouths of tortured spirits, they are not the less poignant.
He stands behind his characters, of whom Villon might have
made one.

Before we are swept away by the intensity of this gamin of
Paris, let us turn back to the words set in the mouth of Bertrans
of Altafort, " Thus is the counterpass observed in me," or to
the lament of Francesca. Whoever cares at all for the art will
remember that the words of this lament sob as branches beaten
by the wind :

> nessun maggior dolore,
> che ricordarsi del tempo felice
> nella miseria ; e ciò sa' l tuo dottore.

The whole sound of the passage catches in the throat, and sobs.
Dante is many men, and suffers as many. Villon cries out as
one. He is a lurid canto of the *Inferno*, written too late to be
included in the original text. Yet had Dante been awaiting the
execution of that death sentence which was passed against him,

although we might have had one of the most scornful denuncia-
tions of tyranny the world has ever known, we should have had
no ballade of stark power to match that which Villon wrote,
expecting presently to be hanged with five companions :

Frères humains qui apres nous vivez.

Men, brother men, that after us yet live,
Let not your hearts too hard against us be ;
For if some pity of us poor men ye give,
The sooner God shall take of you pity.
Here we are, five or six strung up, you see,
And here the flesh that all too well we fed
Bit by bit eaten and rotten, rent and shred,
And we the bones grow dust and ash withal ;
Let no man laugh at us discomforted,
But pray to God that he forgive us all.

II

If we call upon you, brothers, to forgive,
You should not hold our prayer in scorn, though we
Were slain by law ; ye know that all alive
Have not wit alway to walk righteously.[5]

Dante's vision is real, because he saw it. Villon's verse is real,
because he lived it ; as Bertran de Born, as Arnaut Marvoil, as
that mad poseur Vidal, he lived it. For these men life is in the
press. No brew of books, no distillation of sources will match
the tang of them.

[5] Swinburne's translation.

178

IX

THE QUALITY OF LOPE DE VEGA

The art of literature and the art of the theatre are neither identical nor concentric. A part of the art of poetry is included in the complete art of the drama. Words are the means of the art of poetry ; men and women moving and speaking are the means of drama. A play, to be a good play, must come over the footlights.

A composition, so delicate that actual presentation of it must in its very nature spoil the illusion, is not drama. In a play, ordinary words can draw power from the actor ; the words of poetry must depend upon themselves. A good play may, or may not, be literature or poetry. In a study of poetry, one is concerned only with such plays as happen to contain poetry ; in a study of literature, one is concerned only with such plays as may be enjoyably read. The aims of poetry and drama differ essentially in this : poetry presents itself to the individual, drama presents itself to a collection of individuals. Poetry also presents itself to any number of individuals, but it can make its appeal in private, seriatim. Drama must appeal to a number of individuals simultaneously. This requires no essential difference in their subject-matters, but it may require a very great difference in the manner of presentation.

It cannot be understood too clearly that the first requirement of a play is that it hold the audience. If it does not succeed in this it may be a work of genius, or it may be, or contain a number of excellent things, but it is *not* a good play. Some of the means whereby a play holds its audience vary from age to age ; the greater part of them do not. The æsthetic author may complain that these means are mere trickery, but they are in reality the necessary limitations of the dramatic form. They are, for the most part, devices for arousing expectation, for maintaining suspense, or devices of surprise. They are, it is true, mechanical or ingenious, but so is the technique of verse itself.

Rhyme, for instance, is in a way mechanical, and it also arouses expectation—an expectation of the ear for repetition of sound. In the delayed rhyming of Daniel, we have a maintaining of suspense. In every very beautiful or unusual arrangement of words we have " dénouement "—surprise.

The so-called tricks of the stage are its rhymes and its syntax. They are, perhaps, more easily analysed than the subtler technique of lyric poetry, but they cannot be neglected. After these restrictions, or conventions, or laws of the drama have been mastered, the author can add his beauty and his literary excellence. But without these, his excellences are as far from being drama, as a set of disconnected, or wrongly connected wheels and valves, is from being an engine. All great plays consist of this perfected mechanism, plus poetry, or philosophy, or some further excellence which is of enduring interest.

Because it is very difficult to write good poetry, and because the dramatist has so many other means at his command, he usually relapses into inferior poetry or neglects it altogether. When the paraphernalia of the stage were less complicated, this neglect was less easy.

The sources of English drama have been traced by Chambers in his *History of the Mediæval Stage*, to the satisfaction of nearly everyone. In Spain the sources and prime influences of the drama were : the church ceremonies, the elaborate services for Christmas and Easter, which result in the divers sorts of religious plays, saints' plays, and the like ; the dialogue forms of the troubadour poetry, developing in " loas," and " entremes " or skits ; and later, the effect of the travelling Italian company of a certain Ganasa, who brought the " Comedia del Arte " into Spain.

In this " Comedia del Arte " one finds the art of drama, the

art of the stage ; a complete art, as yet unalloyed by any ad-
mixture of the literary art. The comedians chose their subject ;
and each man for himself, given some rough plan, worked out
his own salvation—to wit, the speeches of the character he
represented. That is to say, you had a company of actor-
authors, making plays as they spoke them. Hamlet's " O re-
form it altogether, and let those that play your clowns speak no
more than is set down for them," shows that the effects of this
custom lasted in England until Shakespear's time, at least in
connection with " character " parts.

According to Lope de Vega, "comedies" in Spain are no
older than Rueda. If one is to quibble over origins, one must
name Gomez Manrique (1412–91) as author of liturgical drama
of the simplest sort. He was not the originator, merely the first
author whose name we know ; and Juan del Encina (1468–1534)
for " eclogas " or " skits."

Calisto and Melibea (the " Celestina ") was published 1499 ;
and is probably by Fernando de Rojas. It is a novel in dialogue
of twenty-two acts, unstageable.

The Portuguese, Gil Vincente, lived from 1470–1540 ; it is
not known that his works were ever played in Spain. But
Lope de Rueda (circa 1558), gold-beater, actor-manager, and
playwright, began the theatre.

Whatever may be said to the credit of these originators, there
is no interest except for the special student in any Spanish plays
earlier than those of Lope de Vega,[1] and Lope certainly found
his stage in a much more rudimentary condition than Shakespear
found the stage of England. Whatever be the intrinsic merit of
Lope's work, this much is certain : he gave Spain her dramatic
literature, and from Spain Europe derived her modern theatre.
In his admirable essay on Lope, Fitz-Maurice Kelly says :
" Schiller and Goethe combined, failed to create a national

[1] With the possible exception of one or two plays of Torres Naharro, born
before their due time. I make this exception on the good authority of Mr. Fitz-
Maurice Kelly, as I have not read the plays.

theatre at Weimar ; no one but Lope could have succeeded in creating a national theatre at Madrid."

Shakespear is a consummation ; nothing that is based on Shakespear excels him. Lope is a huge inception ; Calderon and Tirso de Molina, Alarcon, De Castro, have made their enduring reputations solely by finishing what Lope had neglected to bring to perfection. They may excel him in careful workmanship, never in dramatic energy. When I say that Lope's plays are the first which are of general interest, I mean that he is the first who, having mastered the machinery of the drama, added to his plays those excellences which give to his works some enduring interest.

Lope was born 1562, led a varied, interesting life, which is best told by H. A. Rennert in his *Life of Lope de Vega*. He wrote a multitude of miscellaneous works, and from fifteen hundred to two thousand plays, of which about four hundred remain to us. Some of the plays are still as fresh and as actable as on the day they were written.[2] Considering the haste of their composition, it is not remarkable that many others possess merely antiquarian interest. Montalban testifies to Lope's having written fifteen acts in fifteen consecutive days, and many of the plays were probably composed within twenty-four hours.

Lope is bound to the Middle Ages much more closely than are the Elizabethans by reason of his religious plays, a form of art practically uninfluenced by the Renaissance, and already out of fashion in London. Such plays were greatly in demand in Lope's time, and for long after, in Madrid. They attain their highest development at the hands of Calderon. Lope's religious plays scarcely belong to world literature, and it is not on their account that one seeks to resurrect the damaged shade of their author.

From my scant knowledge of the English religious plays, I should say that they are more vigorous than those written in

[2] Echegaray said to me in 1906 : " They are not being played because we haven't the actors. The last actress who could do them is now in South America."

Spanish ; this does not mean that Lope's " obras santos " are without interest, and *El Serafin Humano*, his dramatization of the *Fioretti* of St. Francis is certainly entertaining.

In the opening scenes of the play we find Francisco, an over-generous young man, engaged in a flirtation with certain ladies of no great dignity. These ladies remark among themselves : " Ah, this is a new cock-sparrow ; this will be easy." The ladies' " escudero," or serving-man, proceeds to " work " Francisco for inordinate tips. The lower action runs its course. Francisco gives his clothes to a beggar, and sees a vision ; here the piety of the play begins. Francisco takes the cross ; a " voice " tells him to give up the crusade, that he must fight a better battle where he is ; and in this atmosphere of voices and visions the play proceeds, ending in Brother Gil's vision of the " holy tree."

If Lope's cycle of historical plays do not match Shakespear's cycle of the English kings, it is quite certain that they can be compared to nothing else. From the opening cry in *Amistad Pagada*,

> Al arma, al arma capitanes fuertes,
> Al arma capitanes valerosos,

through the sequence of the plays overflowing the five volumes of Pelayo's huge edition, the spirit of Spain and the spirit of the " romanceros " is set loose upon the boards. It is of " bellicosa Espana," more invincible than " Libia fiera," and of Leon, " already conquered, its walls razed to the ground, coming furious from the mountains."

There is about the cycle no effect of pageantry or of parade ; it is a stream of swift-moving men, intent on action. The scope of the cycle may be judged from the following titles : *King Vamba*, *The Last Goth*, *The Deeds of Bernardo del Carpio's Youth*, *Fernan Gonzalez*, *El Nuevo mondo descubierto por Cristobal Colon*. This last is, I believe, the finest literary presentation of

Columbus known to exist. It is noble and human, and there is admirable drawing in the scene where Columbus is mocked by the King of Portugal. The further main action runs as follows : Bartolomeo brings the news of England's refusal to finance the venture. " Imagination " appears, after the manner of the Greek *deus ex machina* ; and there is a play within the play, a little "morality" of Providence, Idolatry, and Christian religion. Columbus finally gets an audience with King Ferdinand. Fragments of the dialogue are as follows :

> *Colon* :
>> The conquest of Granada brought to happy end,
>> Now is the time to gain the world.
>> . . . .

> The crux ?
>> Lord, money, the money is the all,
>> The master and the north and the ship's track,
>> The way, the intellect, the toil, the power,
>> Is the foundation and the friend most sure.

> *The King* :
>> War with Granada has cost me
>> A sum, which you, perchance, may know.

But the money is finally provided.

Act II opens with the mutiny on shipboard. The eloquence of the strike leaders is of the sort one may hear at Marble Arch on any summer evening.

> *First Mutineers* :
>> Arrogant capitan
>> Of a band deceived,
>> Who in your cause
>> Are nearer unto death
>> Than to the land you seek,
>> Whereto, through thousand thousands
>> Of leagues and of oppressions,
>> You drag them o'er

A thousand deaths to feed
The fishes of such distant seas.
Where's this new world ?
O maker of humbugs,
O double of Prometheus,
What of these dry presages,
Is not this all high sea ?
What of your unseen land,
Your phantom conquest ?
I ask no argosies.
Let go your boughs of gold
And give us barley beards
So they be dry.

The other mutineers continue with ridicule and sarcasm. Frey Buyl saves Columbus, and land is sighted. The third act is of the triumphant return.

Los novios de Hornachuelos (an incident in the reign of Henry III) contains one of the tensest scenes of all romantic drama ; the greater part of this play is delightful comedy : Thus, from Act I, Scene 1 :

Mendo (servant) :
Do you not fear the king ?

Lope Melindez :
The power of the king is not thus great.
My whim serves me for law.
There's no king else for me.
Lope Melindez and none other
Is king in Estremadura.
If Henry gain to rule,
Castile is wide.

Mendo :
You speak notable madness.
Doth not the whole wide world
Tremble for that sick man Henry
Whose valour is past belief.

Melindez threatens his squire, and Mendo replies :

> Those who must please on all occasions must
> be chameleons.
> Must clothe themselves and seem their master's
> colors.

From which lines we learn that the king is an invalid, that Lope Melindez, " the wolf " of Estremadura, is a braggart and rebel, and that his squire is a philosopher in fustian.

Continuing, we find that Melindez has in him " such might of love that he is affrighted of it " ; that there is a gentlewoman called for her beauty the Star, " Estrella " de Estremadura, who is " the cipher of all human beauty." (It is always diverting to notice the manner in which Shakespear and Lope habitually boil down the similes of love into epigrammatic metaphor).

Next a servant announces : " The King-at-Arms of the King," with a letter. Melindez receives him, and says he will reply at leisure. The King-at-Arms replies that the King demands an immediate answer.

> *Melindez* :
> Ah ! punctual fellows,
> The Kings-at-Arms !
>
> *King-at-Arms* :
> Henry
> Doth thee no small honor
> When for Ambassador
> He sendeth such an one as I.
> We Kings-at-Arms
> Move on no lesser service
> Than to bear challenges
> To Emperors or Kings.
>
> *Melindez* :
> The King defies me, then !

The King-at-Arms replies that the King challenges only

equals. The letter is a summons for Melindez to present himself at Court with four servants and no more.

> *Melindez* :
> Oh, Mendo
> I'm for throwing
> This King-at-Arms from a
> Balcony, into the castle moat.
> He becomes too loquacious.

Melindez refuses to obey the summons, makes a long speech to the effect that from his castle, which beholds the sun's birth, he sees no land which hath other lord than himself, and that he has arms for four thousand. After having disburdened himself, he becomes polite, but the King-at-Arms will neither rest nor eat.

> *Melindez* :
> Heaven go with you.

> *King-at-Arms* :
> The King will take satisfaction.

> *Melindez* :
> Sword to sword, let's see
> Who's vassal and who's King !

> (*The King-at-Arms leaves.*)

> *Melindez* :
> I'm for Hornachuelos.

Scene 2 is at Hornachuelos. Estrella enters, and her character is in part shown by her attire. (" Enter Estrella, with javelin, sword, dagger, and plumed sombrero.")

This charming gentlewoman is marrying off a couple of her vassals tenant who have not the slightest desire to be so united. The manner of their unwillingness may be here gathered : (" They take hands without turning round, and Mariana gives Berueco a kick which makes him roll.") Then Mariana :

> I'll give you such a blow
> As will make you spit
> Teeth for two days.

The act ends with a speech of Estrella's :

> Lope Melindez, if love is a flame,
> Then am I snow frozen in the Alps.

In the beginning of the second act the King sees Estrella, and she falls in love with him. The King-at-Arms has delivered Melindez' answer to the King, who rides to Melindez' castle. Then comes the great scene, the duel between two kinds of strength ; it is Lope's thesis for the rights of will and personality.

> *servant* :
> Three horses with riders
> Who would speak with you ;
> One has entered !
>
> *Melindez* :
> Great freedom, by God !
>
> (*King Henry III enters alone.*)
>
> *Henry* :
> Which of the two
> Calls himself Melindez,
> I have wished to know him.
>
> *Melindez* :
> I call myself Melindez.
>
> *Henry* :
> I have a certain business
> Of which I come to speak with you,
> Because I love you.
> It is of importance
> That we be alone.
>
> *Melindez* :
> Leave us.
>
> (*The servants go out.*)

Henry :
Fasten the door.

Melindez :
How fastidious we are !
(*presumably after locking it*)
It is locked.

Henry :
Take this chair, to please me.

Melindez :
I sit.

Henry :
Then listen.

Melindez :
I already listen,
And with wonder.

Henry :
El enfermo rey Enrique[3]

The speech is too long to quote in full. It summarizes the King's reign, begun at the age of fourteen, fraught with all difficulty. It tells of a kingdom set to rights and order drawn from civic chaos, the purport being : such has been my life, such have been its trials ; who are you, Melindez, to stand against me, who to jeopardize the welfare of the kingdom by making it necessary for me to leave it in the hands of subordinates ? The speech ends :

Henry :
. . . Lope Melindez, I am
(*The King here rises from his chair and
  grasps his sword. Lope removes his hat.*)
Enrique, alone we are.
Draw your sword ! for I would
Know between you and me,
Being in your house,
The two of us in this locked room,

---

[3]The sickly King Henry.

Who in Castile deserves
To be king, and who
Wolf-vassal of Estremadura.
Show yourself now to me
Haughty and valorous,
Since you boast so much
In my absence. Come !
For my heart is sound
Though my body be sickly,
And my heart spurts the Spanish blood
Of the descendants of Pelayo !

Melindez :

My Lord, no more,
Your face without knowing you gives terror.
Mad have I been.
Blind I went.
Pardon ! Señor
If I can please you with tears and surrender.
You have my arms crossed.
My steel at your feet,
And my lips also.

(*He casts his sword at the King's feet and kisses the ground.*
(*Henry sets his foot upon Melindez's head.*)

Henry :

Lope Melindez, thus are humbled the gallant necks
    of haughty vassals.

(*The King trembles with the chill of the quartian ague.
He walks.*)

Chance has brought on
The Quartian, have you
a bed near.

Melindez :

In the room below
The floor you tread,
But it's small sphere
For such a sovran king.

Henry :
Open
And tell my servants
To come undress me,
For by my trusted valor
I would pass the night
In your house.

Melindez :
Not in vain
Do the Castillians tremble at you,
O Enrique, terror of the world.

In the third act we return to comedy. The King refuses to marry Estrella, saying among other things that he is an invalid. Estrella and Melindez are ordered to marry each other, and the low-life troubles of Berueco and Mariana are travestied in the higher action. Berueco and Mariana have come to blows ; Estrella and Melindez shoot across the stage playing the same game with swords, Melindez thinking the King has tricked him and Estrella, naturally resenting the insult. The King unravels the entanglement by divorcing the peasants and promising Estrella another husband.

Another delightful play of this historico-romantic sort is *Las Almenas de Toro*. It has an additional interest for us in that Ruy Diaz appears in it, the time treated being slightly earlier than that shown in the *Poema del Cid*.

The play in brief outline is as follows :

King Ferdinand had divided his kingdom at his death, leaving the cities Toro and Zamora to his daughters, Urraca and Elvira. The new King, Sancho, is not content. At the opening of the play we find the King, the Cid, and the Conde Ancures before the gates of Toro, which Elvira has closed through fear of her brother. The Cid advises the King to retire and return unarmed. He advises the King to let the sisters keep their cities. The King rejects this counsel, and the Cid is sent forward as ambassador.

Elvira comes forth upon the city wall, and replies with delightful irony to the King's proposition that she become a nun.

> *Elvira* :
>> Tell him, my Cid,
>> That I have turned Toro into a cloister
>> (Suffice it to see that the gate is well locked.)
>> It is unfitting that a cloister
>> Be opened to a secular person.

The King sees his sister on the battlements, and, without knowing who she is, falls in love with her.

> *The King* :
>> On the battlements of Toro
>> There passed a damozel, or
>> To speak more truly
>> 'Twas the sun's self passed us,
>> Fair the form and light the passing.
>> For her whom I saw on the wall that subtlety wherewith astronomy painteth aloft her divers sights upon the azure mantle of the sky, hath made me such that I believe many imagined things should be true.

The Cid tells him that it is his sister.

> *The King* :
>> An ill flame be kindled in her !

Pastoral action is brought into the play as relief, " contra el arte," as Lope says in his preface.

King Sancho attacks Toro and is repulsed. At the beginning of the second act Bellido Dolfos begins to plot. Then, under cover of night (a purely imaginary night) two soldiers with guitars come out onto the battlements. Lope is constantly opposed to new-fangled scenery and constantly scenic in imagination. Here the soldiers sing while the siege is in progress.

Dolfos, with a thousand men, approaches and pretends to be

Diego Ordonez with relief from Zamora. The ruse succeeds, the town is taken, and Elvira flees.

Dolfos, who had been promised the King's sister in marriage if he took the town, is jealous, and says that the King, or Ancures, or the Cid, has hidden Elvira to cheat him and prevent her marrying below her station. In the meantime the pastoral action runs its course. The Duque de Borgoña, travelling incognito, meets with Elvira, who has disguised herself in country clothing. The people, despite the improbability of the minor entanglement, are convincingly drawn.

Bellido Dolfos finally murders King Sancho. Toro declares for his brother Alfonso, " *el de Leon*," with whom we are familiar in the *Poema*, but Elvira returns, and the town receives her in triumph.

La Estrella de Sevilla is usually listed as a play of the Cloak and Sword. It is also a problem play of advanced disposition. The question set is this : Can a woman marry the man she loves if he have killed her brother, who was his friend ? The King is unjustly angered with Bustos Tabera, the brother, and secretly orders Sancho Ortiz to slay him. Ortiz is bound in duty and honor to obey his King. Lope decides that the marriage is impossible. The handling of royalty in this play is most interesting. The King, Sancho el bravo, is a man subject to the passions, but the incentive to connect evil desire with action comes always from the courtier Arias ; thus the evil proceeds, not from the King, but through him.

In reading a play of Lope's it is always worth while to notice which character precipitates the action. Sometimes the entire movement is projected by the gracioso. In this play Ortiz' serving-man is used solely for comic relief, and with a fine precision. His rôle is very short ; he appears only about eight times, and each time at the exact moment when the tragic strain begins to oppress the audience. Almost imperceptibly he fades out of the play. Lope is past-master of "relief," and here it serves to keep the audience sensitive to the tragic, unjaded.

193

When Ortiz is arrested for murder, he refuses to divulge the cause, and the King is forced to confess that the death is by his order.

Estrella pardons Ortiz, but will not marry him. The dignity of this conclusion is sufficient refutation of those who say that Lope wrote nothing but melodrama, and to please the groundlings.

Three of Lope's surviving plays accord us opportunity for direct comparison with the works of his English contemporaries.

The first is *Castelvines y Monteses*, based on Bandello's novel of *Romeo and Julietta*, and the second, *La Nueva Ira de Dios y Gran Tamorlan de Persia*.

The construction of this play is perhaps more skilful than that of Marlowe's *Tamberlaine*. One misses, I think, the sense of Marlowe's unbridled personality moving behind the words : yet there is a tense vigor of phrase in this play of Lope's, and more lines than one in which Marlowe himself might have poured his turbulence of spirit :

Thus Tamorlan :

> Call me the crooked iron,
> Lame am I and mighty !

And again :

> El mundo mi viene estrecho,
> The world grows narrow for me.

And :

> I've to make me a city
> Of gold and silver, and my house of the bodies of kings,
> Be they rocks of valor.

In the first act we find Bayaceto, the Grand Turk, in love with Aurelia, daughter of the Greek Emperor.

Lope naturally shows us *El Gran Turco* carrying on his courtship *in propria persona* ; strolling in the Emperor's garden in the cool of the day he is taken captive. This imparts a characteristic briskness to the opening scenes of the play. Bayaceto proclaims himself, and is accepted by the Emperor. The betrothal takes place with ceremony.

Tamorlan is increasing in power. Lelia Eleazara, a Turkish lady in love with Bayaceto, curses him at his betrothal. Bayaceto boasts to Aurelia that to please her, he will go out to conquer the world. The passage presumably corresponds to Marlowe's " To entertain devine Zenocrite " and falls below it. News of Tamorlan is brought, and the act closes.

ACT II.

(Sound drums, and in form of squadrons there go forth by one door half the company clad in skins, Tamorlan behind them ; and by the other door the other half, clad as Moors, Bayaceto behind them.)

> *Tamorlan :*
> I am the Tamorlan,
> I am the celestial wrath,
> I am the burning ray,
> Cause of death and dismay
> To whomso looketh upon me
> In mine anger.
> .   .   .   .   .
>
> Son of myself and of my deeds.[4]

Bayaceto is defeated in battle and taken prisoner.

Scene 2. Presumably in the palace of the Emperor.

> *Aurelia (in soliloquy) :*
> Presages sad, how now
> Do ye ill-treat me.
> Meseems ye announce
> Mine end with bale and grief

[4] Hijo de mi mismo y de mis hechos.

> Unto my new-sprung life ;
> Grant comfort,
> Unless my death be fated
> For this day.
> So long the fray !

Aliatar brings news of the battle, with this fine description :

> One sea, fair April
> Mirroring the sky
> With plumes and pennons
> And resplendent arms.

Then, Aurelia, on hearing the outcome,

> No time's for weeping. On !
> Reform our host.
> Call the aged from the farms
> On to Belaquia.
> Homes, lives, and goods
> To bloody smoke be turned,
> Till one flame lap the vale
> That saw the birth
> Of this vile Tamorlan, . . .

Then Elizara comes out, dressed as a madman, and Ozman. Elizara wishes to free Bayaceto by going to Tamorlan disguised as a buffoon.

The next scene shows Tamorlan mocking Bayaceto, in a cage. Elizara enters ; then enter the ambassadors from twenty-nine kings, wishing to ransom Bayaceto : they are refused.

Act III. Tamorlan is overthrown and dies. Elizara becomes a Christian nun.

The play here follows the usual lines of the plays of Spanish and Moorish contest, or the *Chançon de Roland*, for that matter. This sort of conquest play is, of course, no longer suitable for the stage.

Lope's work differs from Shakespear's in that it faces in two directions : thus, *Tamorlan* is a last exhalation of the spirit which produced the " Cantares de Gesta." The saints' plays are a transference to the stage of a literary form which had been long popular. The Spanish historical plays are far more vital than either of these, but their roots are in the older ballades and romances. (The term "romance" is applied in Spanish to a particular form of short narrative poem.) The plays of Lope, which are prophetic of the future stage, are those of the " cloak and sword." The best of which are as fresh and playable today as they were in 1600. It is on this pattern that Beaumarchais has written his *Barber of Seville*, and Shaw his *Arms and the Man*. It is true that Shaw has introduced chocolate creams, and electric bells in Bulgaria, and certain other minor details, but the stock situations and the sprightly spirit of impertinence date at least from Lope. The most diverting proof of this is *El Desprecio Agradecido*, which might have been written —bar certain vagaries of chronos—by Shaw in collaboration with Joachim du Bellay. The action begins with characteristic swiftness.

Personas

DON BERNARDO (from Seville)
SANCHO, his servant
LISARDA, ⎱ sisters
FLORELA, ⎰
INES, their maid
LUCINDO, their brother
DON ALEXANDRO, their father
MENDO, servant of this family
OCTAVIO, betrothed to Lisarda

Acto Primo
(*Come forth Bernardo and Sancho, with drawn swords and bucklers.*)

Bernardo :
  What a rotten jump !
Sancho :
  The walls were high.

Bernardo :
I should have thought you would have leapt the better, since you were the more afraid.

Sancho :
Who isn't afraid of the law, and we just leaving a man dead ?

Bernardo :
Carelessness, I admit. Let who lives, live keenly. It's a fine house we've come into.

Sancho :
I'm flayed entirely. The wall's cost me blood.

Bernardo :
In the darkness I can see no more than that this is a garden.

Sancho :
And what are we going to do about it ?

Bernardo :
To get out, Sancho, is what I should wish to do.

Sancho :
If they hear us, they'll take us for thieves.

Bernardo :
Zeal comes to men in straitened circumstance.

Sancho :
It's the Devil ever made us leave Seville !

Bernardo :
The parlor, shall we go in ?

Sancho :
Yes.

Bernardo :
Women speak.

Sancho :
Notice that they say they are going to bed.

Bernardo :
But what shall we do ?

Sancho :
We shall see what they are, from behind this hanging.

Twenty-eight lines have carried us thus far.
The shifting of the embarrassment indicated in the next to the last line is as keen as it is characteristic.

(Come forth Lisarda, Florela, Ines, and ladies.)

Lisarda :
  Put the light on this table, let me see that tray. Take off these
roses, I don't want them to wither.

Florela :
  How dull Octavio was !

Lisarda :
  There is nothing that bores one so much as a relative ready to
be a husband and not a lover.

Florela :
  Take this chain, Ines . . .

And so on until

(Sancho's buckler falls.)

Lisarda :
  Good Lord ! what's that ?

Florela :
  What fell ?

Ines :
  Don't be afraid.

Lisarda :
  Lock the door, Ines.

Ines :
  Which one ?

Lisarda :
  That which opens into the garden.

Ines :
  It is open.

Lisarda :
  Good care you take (of us) !

Ines :
  We used to lock it later than this.

Lisarda :
  Apologize, and get to work. Take this light, look quickly. What
fell ?

Ines :
  What is this ?

Lisarda :
  How ?

Ines :
  This buckler here !
Lisarda :
  My brother's guard would be like it.
Ines :
  Yes ! And since when have the curtains worn shoes ?
Lisarda :
  Jesus mil veces ! Thieves !

Bernardo comes out, and with eloquent apologies casts himself on their mercy. Lope does justice to the delicate situation. Finally Lisarda says, " Ines, lock them both in this room, and bring me the key " ; and then follows a charming bit of impertinence :

Bernardo :
  Ines, I shall not sleep.
Ines :
  Can you do with this light and a book ?
Bernardo :
  Depends on the book.
Ines :
  Part 26 of Lope.
Bernardo :
  Ajh ! spurious works printed with his name on 'em.

The further entanglement of the comedy is delightful. I have in part explained the characters in the list of *dramatis personæ*.

Bernardo has come from Seville with a letter for Octavio, whose cousin, Bernardo's brother, is about to marry. Octavio hears voices in Lisarda's house on the night of Bernardo's adventure, and is filled with jealousy. When Bernardo, on leaving, delivers his letter and narrates his strange adventures, speaking of the lovely lady and his departure, he says, in Lope's inimitable Spanish :

> Sali, no se si diga enamorado,
> Pero olvidado del amor pasado.

> I came out, I do not know that one would say, in love,
> But forgetful of past love.

Or,

Not enamored, but forgetful of past enamorment.

The cadence and rhyme of the Spanish gives it a certain suavity which I cannot reproduce.

Nothing gives less idea of a play than an outline of its plot : the feelings of Octavio during Bernardo's narration can be readily guessed at, and Lope well displays them.

Both sisters fall in love with Bernardo, and the scene between them reminds one of a similar encounter in Wilde's *Importance of Being Earnest*.

The fact that women were at this time, contrary to the English custom, permitted on the Spanish stage ; and Lope's greater familiarity with the sex, which he married frequently and with varying degrees of formality, accounts for a fuller development of the feminine rôles than one finds in the contemporary English plays. Lope is no mere wit and juggler. Lisarda's speech, when her love for Bernardo seems wholly thwarted by circumstance, brings into the play that poetry which is never far from the pen of " the Phoenix of Spain."

The following translation is appalling in its crudity. Lisarda is walking in the garden where Bernardo had entered the night before :

> Flowers of this garden
> Where entered Don Bernardo
> On whom I look, a sunflower,
> On the sun that is my doom ;
> Rose, carnation, jasmine,
> That with a life securer
> Take joy in your swift beauty,
> Tho' ye make in one same day
> Your green sepulchres
> Of the cradles you were born in ;
> Yet would I speak with you,

Since my joy found beginning
And ending in one day,
Whence took it birth and death,
And I await like ending.
A flower I was as ye,
I was born as ye are born,
And if ye know not rightly
That ye hold your life but lightly,
Learn, O flowers, of me.
The light of your colors,
And the pomp of all your leaves,
The blue, the white, the ruddy,
Paint loves and jealousies.
For this, O flowers, ye pass.
Counsel I give and example.
For yesterday I was, what today I am not,
And if today I am not what I was but yesterday
Now may ye learn from me,
What things do pass away
With the passing of one day.

As ye are, I was certain
That my fair hope would flower.
But love's blossoms alway
Bring forth fruit uncertain.
Aspic living, amor hidden—
Nay, I learnt it not from you—
This killed and said to me:
Whoso look on me now and find me
Changèd so, would not believe
The marvel that I was but yesterday.
Be ye with colors lovely
As those that ye saw love in,
With the perfumed exhalations
That are comets of the flower.
And O, ye easy splendors,
That I stand invoking,
If I be marvellous today,
Consider what yesterday gave shadow
To the sun, with what I was
Who today am not my shadow even.

The play winds on through the comic labyrinths. The man whom Bernardo killed for following his former flame from Seville, turns out not to have been killed, but appears as Lucindo, Lisarda's brother. He and his father try to marry Bernardo to the wrong sister : the marriage of Lisarda to Octavio seems inevitable. Sancho and Mendo, in their love for Ines, parody the main action. The high-flown language of the times' gallantry is mixed with Sancho's cynical matter-of-fact humor. Lope's *graciosos* are often without a sense of humor ; at such times their remarks are usually unconscious, are humorous because of their position in the play : the position of the *gracioso* in Lope's plays is that occupied by Sancho Panza in *Don Quixote*. The chauffeur in Shaw's *Man and Superman* retains some of the *gracioso's* functions. It is part of Lope's mastery of theatrical technique that he seems to whisper privately to each member of his audience, " What fools the rest are ! But *you* and *I* see the thing in its true colors." Thus, to the young romantic, he seems to say, " Behold this gallant, whose nobility and ideals are so misunderstood by his vulgar serving-man " ; and to the *gracioso* in the audience he says, " This ' high falutin' ' romance, these lofty ideals, this code of honor ! What nonsense it is ! " It is flattery, of course, not the subtlest, but practical flattery, harnessed to Lope's theatrical purpose.

Despite their number, Lope's plays are not filled with wooden figures, or masks, or types, but with individuals. There is repetition, small wonder and small harm ; even in Shakespear, Toby Belch and Falstaff are to some extent and much girth the same character.

Any comparison of Shakespear and Lope must be based in part on their distinctly individual treatment of the same theme —that is, Bandello's tale of Romeo and Juliette. The comparison is a fair one, for if *Romeo and Juliet* is not one of Shakespear's greatest plays, it is one-fiftieth part of his work, while Lope's *Castelvines y Monteses* is less than one-fifteen-hundredth part of his.

An English translation of Lope's play by F. W. Cosens appeared in 1869,[5] for private distribution ; this translation should be reprinted, though Cosens is, I think, wrong in attempting a Shakespearian diction in his rendering of Lope's Spanish. Lope's dramatic convention differs from Shakespear's in this : Shakespear's convention is that of ennobled diction. His speech is characteristic of his people, but is more impressive than ordinary speech. Works of art attract us by a resembling unlikeness. Lope's convention is that of rhymes and assonance—that is, his lines differ from ordinary speech in that they are more suave : when Lope becomes ornate, irony is not far distant. The nature of the Spanish language permits rhyme and assonance, without such strain or cramping as these devices would generate in English. His effort is to make speeches which can be more easily pronounced " trippingly on the tongue." Shakespear also aims at this, but it is a secondary aim, and it is concealed by his verse structure, although such words as :

> Nymph, in thy orisons
> Be all my sins
> remembered,

have about them something of the Spanish smoothness. But Lope would have written, I think,

> Nymph,
> In thine orisons
> Be all our sins
> remembered.

Lope is all for speed in dialogue ; his lines are shorter : thus a translation which has his own blemishes, (i.e. those of carelessness), is a truer representation of him than one that retards his action by a richer phrasing. Not that he lacks eloquence or noble diction on occasion, but his constant aim is swiftness.

This criticism must only be applied to certain plays. No formula of criticism even approximately applies to all of Lope's work. What he does today, he does not tomorrow.

[5] Chiswick Press, London.

Dante and Shakespear are like giants. Lope is like ten brilliant minds inhabiting one body. An attempt to enclose him in any formula is like trying to make one pair of boots to fit a centipede.

Lope's *Castelvines y Monteses*, then, lacks Shakespear's richness of diction. He tends towards actual reproduction of life, while Shakespear tends towards a powerful symbolic art. In this play each of the masters has created his own vivid detail. In the Spanish play there is a delightful and continued " double entente " in the garden scene, where Julia sits talking to Octavio, in phrases which convey their real meaning only to Roselo. Shakespear portrays this maidenly subtlety in Act III, Scene 5, in the dialogue between Juliet and her mother.

Although Lope's play ends in comedy, it has a tragic emphasis, no lighter than Shakespear's : thus Julia drinks the sleeping draught, and, as it is beginning to take effect, doubts whether it be not some fatal poison ; so all the fear of death is brought in. Lope is past-master at creating that sort of " atmospheric pressure," which we are apt to associate specifically with Ibsen and Maeterlinck. He envelops his audience with his sense of " doom impending " and his " approach of terror," or in any temper of emotion which most fits his words and makes most sure his illusion.

After Julia has been buried, Roselo comes into the tomb, and the fear of his *criado* (servant), the trusty Marin, in the place of death brings the comic relief.

(In *Los Bandos de Verona*, a later play on this subject by Rojas, the *gracioso* is omitted, and the nurse fills this office in the dramatic machinery, somewhat as the nurse in Shakespear.

Julia awakes ; Marin touches her by accident.

> *Julia* :
>   Man, are you living or dead ?
>
> *Marin* :
>   *Muerto soy* !—Dead am I !

The lovers escape to the country, and live disguised as peasants. Antonio (Julia's father) goes a journey, discovers Roselo, and is about to have him killed, when the voice of his supposedly dead daughter arrests him. The escaped Julia, impersonating her own ghost, terrifies him into forgiveness, and the play ends in restoration and gaiety. There is no absolute stage necessity for the general slaughter at the end of Shakespear's play. If one demand tragedy, Lope creates as intense an air of tragedy in the poison scene above mentioned. A decision as to the relative merits of these two plays depends solely on individual taste ; the greatness of Shakespear is, however, manifest if we shift our ground of comparison to *Acertar Errando*. This play and *The Tempest* are traceable to a common source, presumably of rich beauty. When Furness wrote his introduction to *The Tempest*, no source used by Shakespear in this play had been discovered. *Acertar Errando* is a far more ordinary affair than the English play, but then Lope probably wrote his version in three days or less. In the Spanish play we find a rightful heiress, Aurora Infanta of Calabria, on an island, and early in the course of the play this speech :

> *Aurora* :
> Fabio, Oton, there's a little ship in the offing
> Perplexed and buffeted.
> Proudly the sea with sledgy blows
> Disturbs and drives it on.
> They wait your aid.
> Thus before my eyes
> Die those that clamor there within,
> A prey of the brackish whirl[6]. . .
> The winds play at *pelota* (make them their tennis),
> Ah, boldness little availing !
> Now touch they the stars, and now the sandy floor.

As in the Romeo tale, both authors from their fecundity

[6] *Centro*—trough of the sea.

supply their own detail, never hitting upon the same, but often upon equally enchanting methods of presentation.

Here, I think, we must presuppose much of the beauty to be that of the common source.

The beneficent Prospero is probably Shakespear's own creation, although in Lope's play we find mention of "the power of the stars," and of a "master of the island." I suspect an Italian, and ultimately Oriental, source for both the plays, but this is merest conjecture.

Both Ariel and the phantom music of Shakespear's play were perhaps suggested by Apuleius, but Lope's prince, in describing the tempest, personifies the winds, which had confused his mariners : with common names, to be sure, "Eolo," and "Austro," but it is personification nevertheless. In Lope's *Tarquin* we find a combination of our old friends Stephano and Trinculo : among other things, he, at landing, speaks thus familiarly : "Let me then bless the wine."

Caliban is Shakespear's ; but Lope also mentions an unprepossessing creature, with one eye larger than the other.

Lope's further "enredo" or entanglement differs from that of the English play. He sets fewer characters on the boards, but there is parallel for Ferdinand's imprisonment, and for Sebastian's plot against Alonso (or Caliban's against Prospero— if one choose to regard it so).

In the end the Prince and Island Princess "ascertain by erring," after the manner of such adventure. A separate volume would be required for an adequate academic discussion of this play and the problems it involves.

One might continue giving synopses of Lope's plays almost *ad infinitum*. No formula of criticism is, as I have said, of any great use in trying to define him. He is not a man, he is a literature. A man of normal energy could spend a fairly active life in becoming moderately familiar with the 25 per cent. of Lope's work which has survived him.

His *Adonis y Venus* does not seem particularly happy ; it is perhaps typical of his dramatic treatment of classic themes. But if these imitations are without notable value, how gladly do we turn to those shorter poems, which are really Spanish. Thus :

> A mis soledades voy
> De mis soledades vengo
> Porque para andar conmigo
> Mi bastan mis pensamientos.

The true poet is most easily distinguished from the false, when he trusts himself to the simplest expression, and when he writes without adjectives.

> To my solitudes I go,
> From my solitudes return I,
> Sith for companions on the journey,
> Mine own thoughts (do well) suffice me.

These lines are at the beginning of some careless redondillas, representing the thoughts he takes with him journeying ; among which this quatrain :

> Envy they paint with evil chere,
> But I confess that I possess it,
> For certain men who do not know
> The man that lives next door to them.

He is ever at these swift transitions. I think his thoughts outran even his pen's celerity, so that often he writes only their beginnings. It is this that gives him buoyancy, and inimitable freshness. For, notwithstanding the truth of Fitzmaurice Kelly's statement that in his non-dramatic work " Lope followed everyone who made a hit," there is about his plays nothing *fin de siècle*, but always an atmosphere of earliest morning. There is no kind of excellence (except that of sustained fineness) of which we dare say, " it was beyond him," since our refutation may be concealed anywhere in those surviving plays of his, which no living man has read.

Hood's delicacy in one corner of his mind, in another, the vigor of Marlowe. If haste or love of words has left some of his nature painting rhetorical, his

> *A penas Leonora*
> *La blanca aurora*
> *Puso su pie de marfil*
> *Sobre las flores de Abril,*

> Scarcely doth the white dawn press
> Her ivory foot upon the April flowers,

is as descriptive of the pale dawn of Spain as is Shakespear's " in russet mantle clad," of the more northern day's approaching.

As illustration of his suave, semi-ironical gallantry I quote this from a passage between " galan " and " gracioso."

> *Galan :*
> Porque eso nombre mi dan ?
> *Gracioso :*
> No vienes desde Milan
> Solo a ver un mujer ?
> *Galan :*
> No es una mujer mas que una ciudad
> Siendo un mundo de pesar
> Siendo un cielo de plazer ?

> *Master :*
> Why do they give me this name (*i.e.* fool) ?
> *Man*
> Didn't you come all the way from Milan
> Just to look at a woman ?
> *Master :*
> Isn't a woman more than a city,
> Being a world of trouble
> And a heaven of pleasure ?

Between his vigor and his suavity, his wit and his tenderness, the intoxication grows within one. One may know him rather well and yet come upon him suddenly in some new phase; thus, if one knows only his irony, one comes upon the slumber song in the little book of devotions, *Los Pastores de Belen* (*The Bethlehem Shepherds*). One stanza is as follows, the Virgin singing it :

> Cold be the fierce winds
> Treacherous round him ;
> Ye see that I have not
> Wherewith to guard him.
> O Angels, divine ones
> That pass us a-flying ;
> Sith sleepeth my child here
> Still ye the branches.

If we at this late day are bewildered at his versatility, it is small wonder that the times which saw the man himself should have gone mad over him.

It is not in the least surprising that in 1647 there should have appeared a creed beginning " I believe in Lope de Vega the Almighty, the poet of heaven and earth " ; the marvel is that the Inquisition should have been able to suppress it.

A Spaniard told me not long since that Lope prophesied the wireless telegraph. I have forgotten the exact passage which he used as substantiation, but I am quite ready to believe it.

At the end of this century Lope's works may be reasonably accessible. The best English sources of information concerning Lope are : H. A. Rennert's *Life of Lope de Vega* ; Fitzmaurice Kelly's essay on Lope, in his *Chapters on Spanish Literature* ; and the pages on Lope in his *History of Spanish Literature*. Synopses of a number of plays are given in A. F. Von Schack's *Geschichte des dramatischen Literatur und Kunst in Spanien*. There is a Spanish translation of this work by E. de Mier.

Anyone who can read Spanish would do well to apply himself to the plays themselves.

No prince of letters ever ruled such subjects as had Frey Lope Felix de Vega y Carpio.

Either Cervantes or Calderon would have made a great age of letters.   Quevedo, Herrera, and a score of other notable poets are scarcely known outside the Spanish-speaking countries and the cliques of Spanish scholars.   The histories give us catalogues of their works, but convey no idea of their flavour.   Such collections as are available are for the most part the choice of Eighteenth Century critics, and do not represent the spirit of the spacious days.

Few poets have known better the beautiful way of words than did Fernando Herrera.

Quevedo's fancy could bring forth conceits such as that to his lady looking into a fountain :

> Las aguas que han pasado
> Oiras por este prado
> Llorar no haberte visto con tristeza.
> You may hear the waters that have passed,
> A-weeping through the meadows,
> That they have not seen you.

And if one love Wordsworth's " the world is too much with us," one must care also for Quevedo's ode beginning,

> Alexis, what contrary
> Influence of heaven
> Persecutes our souls
> With the things of the world.

1929 : Perhaps the best diagnosis I can now find is that unless one apply the very strict standards formulated in my opening essay there is a great deal of Spanish poetry, both lyric and dramatic, which will satisfy the lovers of " poetic " ornament. The sound of the language is richer than that of Ariosto's.   There is a vast mass of Seventeenth Century Spanish poetry quite as good as most of the Italian and English " poetry " found in standard collections. A good deal of it is Italian in origin. The real kick is found in the Spanish short narrative " ballads " which are Spanish and nothing but Spanish. " Renaissancism " continued in Spain down to Campoamor, and I don't imagine his lone spurt finished the general flow.

Perhaps the atmosphere in which this Spanish drama was presented may be suggested by this quotation from a book of travels, published thirty years after Lope's death.

The book is, I believe, quite common, but the one copy which I saw in Madrid had no author's name on the title page, in consequence of which I have not been able to find it in any library. *Voyage d'Espagne, curieux, historique et politique* ; *fait en l'année* 1665. Paris : Chez Charles de Lerey.

" On the 27th of May we were present at ' the fiesta' of Corpus, the most ' ostentiosa' and largest of all that we observed in Spain. It commenced with a procession, preceded by a great number of musicians and ' vizcainos' with tambourines and castanets. There accompanied them, moreover, many other persons with garments more befitting, leaping and dancing as it had been carnival, in time to the instruments.

The King went to the church Santa Maria, nearest the palace, and after hearing mass, returned with a candle in his hand.

Before was borne the tabernacle, followed by ' grandees' of Spain, and the divers ' consejos' (orders) mingled in disorder on this day to escape disputes of pre-eminence. With the first of the accompanying company were to be observed moreover giant machines, that is, figures of pasteboard, which moved by the efforts of men hidden in them.

They were of divers forms and some horrible, all representing women, save the first, which is a monstrous head, painted and placed upon the shoulders of a ' devoto' of small stature, in such a manner that the combination resembles a dwarf with the head of a giant. There are beside other horrors, of like sort, representing two giants, the one, ' moro' (moor, brown), and the other black. The people call these figures " Los hijos del Vecino."

They told me also of another like figure which passes through the streets, and is called ' La Tarasca.' This name, as it is said, cometh from a bosque that existed of old in ' La Provenza,' in the place where lieth Tarascon or Beaucaire, over against Roldano. It is asserted that in a certain time it was dwelt in by a serpent, as hostile to the human race as was that one which was the cause of our first parents being sent from Paradise. Santa Marta at last did him to death by virtue of her orisons, ' oraciones' (preaching ?), and hung him by her girdle.

Be there what may in this tradition, this which is called ' La Tarasca,' to which I refer, is a serpent of monstrous magnitude, with enormous belly, long neck, smallish feet, pigeon-toed, eyes threatening, and jaws horrible, prominent and thrust forward ; its body is sewed with scales.

They bear this figure through the streets, and those who are hidden beneath the cardboard that forms it, direct it to make such movements that they knock off the hats from the heads of the unheeding.

The simple folk hold it in great fear, and when it catches one, it causes thunderous laughter among the spectators. The most curious thing of all was the obeisance that these ' monigotes ' make to the Queen, when the procession passes the balcony which she occupies. Moreover, the King did his obeisance unto the Queen ; she and the Infanta descend from their seats ; the procession then took its way to the Plaza (Mayor ?), and returned to Santa Maria by the Calle Mayor. From this time to the fifth hour of the afternoon are represented ' autos.' They are religious dramas, among which are interspersed burlesque ' entremeses ' to mitigate and give spice to the seriousness of the show.

The companies of players, of which there are two in Madrid, close the theatres at this time for the space of more than a month, and put only religious pieces on the boards.

They are obliged to play daily before the house of one of the ' presidentes del consejo.' The first function is celebrated before the royal palace, where there is raised for this purpose a booth with a ' dias,' beneath which sit their majesties. The theatre extends to the foot of the throne. In place of the green-room they have closets on wheels. In place of scenery they use properties on wheels, from behind which come forth the actors, and whither they retire at the end of each scene. Before beginning the ' autos,' the dancers of the procession and the ' monigotes ' of pasteboard referred to, show their tricks in the presence of the people. That which disturbed me most, most surprised me in the representation of an ' auto,' at which I was present in ' El prado viejo ' (old meadow), was that presenting the play in the middle of the street, and by the light of day they burned ' luces,' while in other closed theatres they make use of the natural light, without using the artificial."

X

In 1453 Constantinople was captured by Mohamed II, " conqueror of two empires, twelve kingdoms, and three hundred cities." This event and the invention of printing did not cause the Renaissance, but precipitated it. During the dark ages there had been a series of attempts ; of abortive Renaissances ; Charlemagne, Alfred, Alcuin, Rosclin, Abelard, the so-called awakening in the Tenth Century and in the Twelfth, Petrarch, and Boccaccio, all precede that period which is termed the Renaissance. But without the printing press, or without such trained slaves to multiply manuscripts, as there had been for the publishers of Imperial Rome, there could be no victory over the general ignorance ; no propagandist movement could be more than local or temporary.

The fall of the city of Constantine scattered classical scholars and manuscripts over Europe ; and coupled with other Moslem conquests, closed the old caravan routes, making it necessary, if trade with the East one must, to trade by some other way ; whence the doubling of the Cape of Good Hope, and the discovery of America ; whence the sense of expansion which is mirrored in literature, usually in a style showing to greater or less degree the influence of the Greek or Roman classics. Thought was supposedly set free, but style was taken captive, for an age at least.

Shakespear is the consummation : in most of his work traces of means have to a large extent disappeared. Lope is, in part, of the Middle Ages ; in part, of the mid-stream of the Renaissance ; and, in part, a result of it.

Both Lope and Shakespear add their incalculable selves to any expression of the Time Spirit ; they owe much to it, but are not wholly dependent. Till now we have treated only of the generative forces in literature : Camoens is not a force, but a symptom. His work is utterly dependent upon the events and temper of his time ; and in it, therefore, we may study that temper to advantage. A corresponding study in architecture were a study of " barocco."

Os Lusiadas is, according to Hallam, " the first successful attempt in modern Europe to construct an epic poem on the ancient model." The subject fits the time ; it is the voyage of Vasco de Gama, with the history of Portugal interpolated. This voyage was made in 1497-1499. Camoens was born in 1524, and *The Portuguese* (*Os Lusiadas*) published in Lisbon in 1572.

We are summoned to attend this song in a style grandiloquent, flowing, " Hum estylo grandiloquo e corriente," because it tells of real men, whose deeds surpass all the fictitious deeds of fabled heroes.

The quality of Camoens' mind is rhetorical, but his diction and his technique are admirable. The beauty of Camoens will never be represented in English until his translators learn to resist translating every Portuguese word by an English word derivative from the same Latin root. The translation of Camoens into words of Saxon origin would demand a care of diction equal to that of the author, and would retain the vigor of the original. A translation filled with Latinisms looks like a cheap imitation of Milton ; and if one wants a Miltonic version of the grand style of Portugal, one had much better go to Milton himself, to passages like the following :

> As when to them who sail
> Beyond the Cape of Horn, and now are past
> Mozambic, off at sea north-east windes blow
> Sabean odors from the spicie shore
> Of Arabie the blest, with such delay
> Well pleased they slack their course, and many a league
> Cheared with the grateful smell, old ocean smiles.

Camoens writes resplendent bombast, and at times it is poetry. The unmusical speech of Portugal is subjugated, its many discords beaten into harmony. As florid rhetoric, the *Lusiads* are, I suppose, hardly to be surpassed. The charm is due to the vigor of their author, his unanimity, his firm belief in the glory of externals ; and there is also a certain pleasure in coming into contact with Camoens' type of mind, the mind of a man who has enthusiasm enough to write an epic in ten books without once pausing for any sort of philosophical reflection. He is the Rubens of verse.

An epic cannot be written against the grain of its time : the prophet or the satirist may hold himself aloof from his time, or run counter to it, but the writer of epos must voice the general heart. Although Camoens is indubitably a poet, one reads him today with a prose interest. *Os Lusiadas* is better than an historical novel ; it gives us the tone of the time's thought. Thus far it is epic. By its very seeming faults it shows us what things interested the people of that time.

Geography, as fresh then as is aviation today, could be dwelt upon at length ; the costumes of people in strange places were worth description.

This much is real ; the furniture of deities is a nuisance, but the real weakness of the Lusiads is that it is the epic of a cross section, and voices a phase, a fashion of a people, and not their humanity.

Apart from the prose interest, our interest is in his use of language. What Camoens wanted is very clearly stated in Book I, Stanza 5 :

> Give me a madness great and sounding,
> Not of the country pipe or shepherd's reed.
> But of a trumpet resonant and warlike.[1]

The muses answered his prayers with precision. He got his

---

[1] Mas de tuba canora e bellicosa.

trumpet, and his wind was excellent. As his beauty depends solely on his diction and sound, great care must be taken in translation, or nothing remains but rhetoric. His technique may be proven by a few illustrations, and the dangers of careless translation likewise. Thus, of committing the ships to the sea :[2]

> commetando
> O duvidoso mar n' hum lenho leve.
> Unto the doubtful sea their wood unweighty.

Half the charm of the line is in the assonance.

His simplicity and directness are greater than anyone would suppose from any translation that I have seen. Aubertin, attempting to retain the original rhyme scheme, renders :

> Da lua os claros raios rutilavam[3]
> Pelas argenteas ondas neptuninas.
> Now did the moon in purest lustre rise
> On Neptune's silvery waves her beams to pour.

Literally :

> The clear rays of the moon glitter
> Through the argent waves of the sea.

(We have no English adjective " neptunian.")

The lines following are as free from ornateness :

> The stars accompany the heavens
> As a field reclothed with daisies,
> The furious winds rest in the dark, strange caves.[4]
> But the folk of the fleet keep vigil,
> As for long time had been their wont.

In Canto I, line 59, we find the words " aurora marchetada." The dictionaries give " marchetar," to inlay, enamel, adorn ;

[2] *Os Lusiadas*, I, 27.
[3] *Os Lusiadas*, I, 58, 1–2.
[4] (*Perigrinas*—caves where even they come as strangers.)

but " marcheta " is a mantle, or that part of a mantle, or man-
tilla, where the ribbons are fastened.   Thus it is obvious, both
for sense and for beautiful association, that we must not translate " aurora marchetada " as enamelled, or even adorned
Aurora, but :

> The mantled (or even, beribboned) dawn
> Spreads out her glorious hair
> Upon the sky serene, opening the ruddy door
> To clear Hyperion, awakened.
> All the fleet began to " embanner " itself,
> And to adorn itself, with joyful awnings,
> To receive with festivities and joy
> The ruler of the isles who was departing.

Modern interest in the poem centers in the stanzas of the
third canto which treat of Ignez da Castro.   The tale of Ignez
will perhaps never be written greatly, for art becomes necessary
only when life is inarticulate and when art is not an expression,
but a mirroring, of life, it is necessary only when life is apparently
without design ; that is, when the conclusion or results of given
causes are so far removed or so hidden, that art alone can show
their relation.   Art that mirrors art is unsatisfactory, and the
great poem, " Ignez da Castro," was written in deeds by King
Pedro.   No poem can have as much force as the simplest
narration of the events themselves.

In brief : Constança, wife of Pedro, heir to the throne of
Portugal, died in 1345.   He then married in secret one of her
maids of honor, Ignez da Castro, a Castilian of the highest rank.
Her position was the cause of jealousy, and of conspiracy ;
she was stabbed in the act of begging clemency from the then
reigning Alfonso IV.   When Pedro succeeded to the throne,
he had her body exhumed, and the court did homage, the
grandees of Portugal passing before the double throne of the
dead queen and her king, and kissing that hand which had been
hers.   A picture of the scene hangs in the new gallery at Madrid,

in the series of canvasses which commemorate the splendid horrors of the Spanish past.

Camoens, for once unadorned, begins his allusion with four immortal lines :

> O caso triste, e digno de memoria
> Que do sepulchro os homes desenterra
> Aconteceo da miseria, e mesquinha
> Que, despois de ser morta foi Rainha.

> A sad event and worthy of Memory,
> Who draws forth men from their closed sepulchres,
> Befell that piteous maid, and pitiful
> Who, after she was dead was crownèd queen.

I have had to add " closed " and " crownèd " to keep the metre. The powerful antithetic suggestion of the second line can escape no one.

The further narrative, with the comparison to the wilted daisy, is beautiful and full of music ; but it is the beauty of words and cadences, and of expression, not the beauty of that subtler understanding which is genius, and the dayspring of the arts. How wise is De Quincey, when he speaks of the " miracle which can be wrought simply by one man's feeling a thing more keenly, understanding it more deeply, than it has ever been felt before." In this pass fails Camoens, for all his splendor, and with him fail the authors of the Renaissance. It is true that he felt the glory of Portugal as no other poet has felt it. But this glory was short-lived.

Every age, every lustrum, yields its crop of pleasant singers, who know the rules, and who write beautiful language and regular rhythms ; poetry completely free from the cruder faults : but the art of writing poetry which is vitally interesting is a matter for masters. The above has for so long been platitude that no one recognizes more than the surface of it.

Those who enjoy the submarine parts of Keats' *Endymion*

will probably enjoy, for contrast and comparison, that part of
the sixth canto of *Os Lusiadas* which treats of Bacchus' visit to
Neptune.

> No mas interno fundo das profundos
>   Cavernas altas, onde o mar se esconde
> La donde as ondas sahem furibundas
>   Quando as iras do vento o mar responde.

There is a fine thunderous resonance about it.

> In th' inmost deep of the profound
> High caverns, where the sea doth hide him,
> There, whence the waves come forth in madness,
> When to the wraths of wind the sea respondeth.

Here dwells the lord of the trident ; behind golden gates
inlaid with seed pearl ; and here is the gentle reader introduced
to all the deities, and demi-deities, whose acquaintance he has
not already made in the lofty courts of Jove.

Nowhere, I think, does Camoens reach the Miltonic maxi-
mum of twenty-four allusions to the classics and Hebrew
Scriptures, in a passage of twenty lines.

In brief, then, *The Lusiads* is remarkable as the sustained
retention of an assumed grand manner. Camoens was a master
of sound and language, a man of vigor and a splendid rhetori-
cian ; that part of the art of poetry which can be taught, he
learned. Longfellow had the same type of mind. Marooned
on a stern and rock-bound coast, planted in an uninteresting
milieu, and in a dreary age, Camoens would have shown a
corresponding mediocrity. If in the future anyone should ever
become interested in the mid-eighteenth-century atmosphere of
Massachusetts, he would find the works of Longfellow most
valuable as archæological documents. Thus, to the student of
the Renaissance, Camoens.

Robert Garnett's translation of some of his sonnets is a labor
of love, and may convey a more favorable impression.

If one were seeking to prove that all that part of art which is not the inevitable expression of genius is a by-product of trade or a secretion of commercial prosperity, the following facts would seem significant. Shortly before the decline of Portuguese prestige, Houtman, lying in jail for debt at Lisbon, planned the Dutch East India Company. When Portugal fell, Holland seized the Oriental trade, and soon after Roemer Visscher was holding a salon, with which are connected the names of Rembrandt, Grotius, Spinoza, Vondel (born 1587) " the one articulate voice of Holland," Coornhert, Spieghel, Coster, Hooft, Raeel, Vossius, Erasmus, and Thomas-à-Kempis.

Our interest centers in the work of Vondel, whose plays and whose non-dramatic work reflect not only these forces of the Renaissance which we have already noted, but also the forces of the religious struggle then in progress. The one play which I know to be available for those who do not read Dutch is the *Lucifer*, translated by Leonard van Noppen. Van Noppen's introductory essay on *Vondel's Life and Times* repays the reading. I can illustrate what I find lacking in Camoens—which is, I suppose, nothing more or less than the magical quality of poetry—by one line from Lope. It is in his *La Circe*, written, presumably, in emulation of Camoens' " hit," *The Lusiads*, where he speaks of " The white forest of the Grecian ships."[5]

Perhaps Camoens may be tried in an easier fire and found wanting. Let us test him with two lines of that modern Italian whose beautiful cold intellect we, outside of Italy, are so slow in praising.

> Come in chiare acque albor lontan di stella
> Ridea l'alma ne gli occhi e trasparia.[6]

Her soul smiles in her eyes and shows through them
As the far whiteness of a star in clear waters.

[5] De Griegas naves una blanca selva.
[6] Carducci : *Juvenalia*, I, xl.

The practical failure of Carducci to get a hearing outside the most cultured and fastidious circles of Italy is a striking proof that poetry is something more than exquisite thought.

If poetry be a part of literature—which I am sometimes inclined to doubt, for true poetry is in much closer relation to the best of music, of painting, and of sculpture, than to any part of literature which is not true poetry ; if, however, Arnold considered poetry as a part of literature, then his definition of literature as " criticism of life " is the one notable blasphemy that was born of his mind's frigidity.

The spirit of the arts is dynamic. The arts are not passive, nor static, nor, in a sense, are they reflective, though reflection may assist at their birth.

Poetry is about as much a " criticism of life " as red-hot iron is a criticism of fire.

XI

The cult of Provence was, as we have said, a cult of the emotions ; that of Tuscany a cult of the harmonies of the mind. The cult of the Renaissance was a cult of culture.

It is probably true that the Renaissance brought in rhetoric, and all the attendant horrors. Between the age of Dante and the age of Shakespear none sang as did the contemporaries of these men. The difference between the songs of their periods is due to the fact that there had been a Renaissance. The " sense of expansion " affects the spirit of song primarily : the influence of the classics bears primarily upon the style. If we are to learn the exact nature of this influence, we must examine those works where it appears least affected by other influences—that is, the works of the men who were the most persistent in their effort to bring the dead to life, and who most conscientiously studied and followed their models. The men who wrote in the mother-Latin have the best of it, since in them alone does the inner spirit conform to the outward manner. They alone do no violence to their medium ; their diction is not against the grain of the language which they use. In these men dwelt the enthusiasm which set the fashion ; their myths and allusions are not a furniture or a conventional decoration, but an interpretation of nature. The classical revival was beneficent in so far as it broke down the restricting formulæ of mediæval art, and it brought back to poetry a certain kind of nature-feeling which had been long absent.

Parenthesis, 1929. One is now pretty well stumped to know just what this benefit may have been. The sense of expansion possibly made the drama. It is equally possible that the gain to poesy was nil. I mean to poetry as poetry, though the art couldn't have remained

223

stationary. Whatever advances have been made in the art of living or the art of envisaging life, have been via a series of approaches to the classic *Anschauung* ; and in that process we have had gradually to reject almost everything " artistic " invented after 1527, especially anything labled " classic " in any of the since-then-labled classic periods.

The best Latin was written in Italy, and if the men who wrote it were not immortals, they were at least sincere, and they sang of the things they cared about.

I can place over the collections of Toscanus and Gherus, and over the period of Latin singing represented therein, no more fitting inscription than Andrea Navgeri's rune for a fountain :

Inscriptio Fontis

Lo ! the fountain is cool and
      none more hale of waters.
Green is the land about it,
      soft with the grasses.
And twigged boughs of elm
      stave off [1] the sun.

There is no place more charmed
      with light-blown airs,
Though Titan in utmost flame
      holdeth the middle sky,
And the parched fields burn with
      the oppressing star.

Stay here thy way, O voyager,
      for terrible is now the heat ;
Thy tired feet can go no further now.
Balm here for weariness is
      sweet reclining,
Balm 'gainst the heat, the winds,
      and greeny shade !
And for thy thirst the lucid fount's assuaging.

[1] Arceo.

Ercole Cuccoli, in his " Studio," on Mark Anthony Flaminius (Bologna, 1897), quotes Carducci to the effect that, " a denial of the æsthetic fineness of a no small part of the poetry, Italian *and Latin*, of the Cinquecento cannot be made except with great injustice, or by one who has an inadequate knowledge of art."

Cuccoli follows this by saying, " everyone recognizes the *period*, but what is lacking is a careful study of the *works themselves*."

Presuming on the part of the reader a certain familiarity with the times of Raphael and Buonarroti, I proceed with notice of the man whose words I have above translated, Andrea Navgeri : " from Sabellico in the Venitian province, a man profiting by Latin letters and by Greek, a pupil of Marcus Musorus, in Latin diction and in observation surpassing his preceptor."

" To the Winds " he makes this *Prayer for Idmon* :

> Ye winds that cross the air
> > on light-plumed wing
> And murmur gentle-voicèd
> > through deep groves ;
> These garlands Idmon
> > giveth you,
> Idmon, the rustic, scattereth
> > to you
> This basket full of
> > fragrant crocuses,
> Make temperate the summer's heat,
> > bear off the useless chaff,
> While 'neath the mid-day
> > he faneth the grain.

One is reminded of Joachim du Bellay's song of the *Winnowers of Wheat to the Winds*, and, indeed, the work of these Italians writing in Latin is not unlike that of the French Pléiade. It was written first and the Pléiade were not unfailingly ignorant of it. Navgeri, again, voices the feeling of the risorgimento in the inscription for

The Image of Pythagoras

He who, Fame saith, hath lived so oft a soul re-born,
Into a changèd body oft returning.
Behold ! once more from heaven
He comes and through Asyla's skill hath life,
And serves the ancient beauty with his lineament.

Some worthy thing he broodeth certainly,
So stern of brow, so mightily withdrawn within himself,
He could the high perceptions of the soul show forth were't not
That held from the older cult, he doth not speak.[2]

In the last line, " silet " suggests the " silentes anni " of the Pythagorean disciples.

The lament of Baldassare Castiglione (that " courteous prince of Mantua, *civitium ocelle*, known to all as the author of *Il Cortegiano*) for the painter whom he loved, re-echoes the spirit of the times' desire.

De Morte Raphaelis Pictoris
(transcription of part of the poem)

Unto our city Rome, sore wounded
By the sword and flame and flow of years,
Thou did'st bring back that rare, lost beauty
That was hers of old. Did'st scorn
The laws that bind us lesser mortals
And dared'st lead back a soul unto its earthly dwelling,
And the spirit unto this our poor dead city ;
Wherefore were the very high gods angry
With thee, O Raphael, and took thee from us
While thy years were yet as flowers.

The reference to restoring Rome's lost beauty does not, in all probability, refer to Raphael's painting, but to a certain matter of which he had written to the Count Baldassare in these words :

[2] Sed veteri obstrictus religione, silet.

His Holiness, in doing me honor, has laid a heavy burden upon my shoulders, which is the care and charge of building St. Peter's . . . the model I have made pleases his Holiness. . . . I would fain find out the fine forms of the antique buildings. . . . I do not know whether I am attempting to fly like Icarus. . . . Vitruvius gives me great light but not sufficient.

Of the men whose fame rests, or might rest chiefly on their Latin poems, the best known is Marcus Antonius Flaminius, born in 1498 in Serravalle. Until the age of fourteen he studied with his father, John Flaminius, superintendent of schools in Serravalle ; "a man of Spartan simplicity," author of *The Lives of the Roman Emperors* and *Lives of the Dominican Saints* ; one "shunning the glamor of the papal court," to which, however, he sends young Mark at the tender age of sixteen, armed with the family's poetical works, and an introduction to Leo X. Authors, especially Latin poets, seem, in the Cinquecento, to have been born—or made—collectively ; thus we have five Capilupi, three Amalthei, Castiglione and his wife, and other combinations.

At the papal court young Mark was favorably received by the Pope and his cardinals. One says that he was "learned and awkward," another that he was "amiable and bashful," while the Cardinal of Aragon, "charmed with his manners and talent," says that Mark fearlessly disputed with the Pontiff himself.

In the poems of Mark Antony Flaminius we find signs of the scholar's sensitiveness to nature, both to the natural things themselves and to those spiritual presences therein, which age after age finds it most fitting to write of in the symbolism of the old Greek mythology. Gently and sincerely religious, we find Flaminius the friend of most of the brilliant men in Italy ; among these were Valdez, the Spanish reformer, and Cardinal Pole. His religious quality, or the quality of his religion, can be seen in his *Hymnus III* :

Ut flos tenellos, in sinu
Telluris almae, lucidam
Formosus explicat comam
Si ros et imber educat
Illum : tenella mens mea
Sic floret, almi spiritus
Dum rore dulci pascitur
Hoc illa si caret, statim
Languescit ut flos arida
Tellure natus, eum nisi
Et ros et imber educat.

Hymn III

As a fragile and lovely flower unfolds its gleaming foliage on the breast-fold of the fostering earth, if the dew and rain draw it forth ; thus doth my tender mind flourish if it be fed with the sweet dew of the Fostering Spirit.

Lacking this, it straightway beginneth to languish even as a flower born upon dry earth, if the dew and the rain tend it not.

This prose translation is modelled upon that in the *Scholar's Vade Mecum*, by John Norton, an odd, egotistical little book printed in 1674.

A certain E. W. Bernard translated fifty of Flaminius' poems during the first quarter of the last century, but there is as yet no representative English version of them.

For the pagan side of Flaminius' poetry, I give you one simile from the *Hercules and Hylas*, where Hylas, " being a-wandered in the silent hills," comes to the " fountain filled with little gleamings." The nymphs seize him and bear him quickly away beneath the waters.

As once in the splendor of the spring-time
A flying star drooped through the gloom of the night
Shone forth, then sank in the sea-deep.

The nature-worship and the abandonment of the chivalric love mode, which mark the definite break with mediæval tradition, are easily perceptible in the following fragments of Flaminius :

To the Dawn

Behold from the Earth's rim cometh Eoe !
Aurora resplendent draweth the rose of her chariot,
In her flushed bosom she bears the far-gleaming light.
Be gone ye wan shades unto Orcus !
Be gone ye dread faces of the manes
Who all night long bring to me dreams and foreboding.
Now bring the bard his lyre, slave,
And scatter flowers while I sing :
' *Salve, Bona Diva,*' thou that makest luminous
Dark lands with the might of thy splendor.
Thine are the fragile violets and crocuses !
Thine are the wicker baskets of fragrant Amomon !
The wind ariseth and beareth to thee our sweet perfumes
. . . .

Goddess fairer than all other goddessess,
Rose-cheeked, when thou dost spread forth
Thy golden hair along the sky
Then flee the tawny stars,
The moon's pale beauty wanes.
Lacking thee were all things lacking color,
And mortals were buried in gloom,
Nor would our life bear flower in the skilful arts.
Thou drivest sleep from our sluggard eyes,
Sleep that is image of Lethe.

In another poem of the night is the following :

It thunders, the grove groaneth for the greatness of the wind, the multitude of the rains pour down. Night with her sleep-bearing winds is round about us, and is blind. The cloak of strange cloud-forms makes dark the earth.

Flaminius loves the feel of the elements ; he knows also that the land he dwells in is haunted by the shades of those Roman

singers from whom he has learned his ways of song ; whence
this to the haunts of Catullus :

> O pleasing shore of Sirmio,
> White-shining hill of Catullus !
> O Muse, teach me to sing the praise
> Of the blest sylvan ways
> Citrus laden, and of Lesbia the fair.
> Stands an altar to thee
> In the flower-filled vale of Taburnus
> Green and cut from the turf.
> Thrice from the foam-filled bowl we pour
> Thee milk, and thrice of the honey's store.
> Suppliant our voices call thee,
> Goddess, to an unskilled sacrifice,
> That thy reed pipe sweetly tuned may
> Sing for her, the fairest maid of all the meadland,
> Our Hyellas.

The complete difference between the love modes of Tuscany
and Provence and those of the classic revival can be seen in the
following *genre*.

> May the mother of love be tender, granting thee youth forever,
> With thy cheek's bloom unfurrowed.
> When after the day's last meal with thy mother and sweet Lycinna,
> Mayst thou visit my mother, Pholoe beloved,
> And together we will watch by the great fire,
> And that night shall be fairer than the day's fairness.
> While the old wives tell their tales over,
> While little Lycinna roasts her chestnuts,
> We will sing gay songs together.

The nature feeling is present in Camillus Capilupus' song to
the night :

Ad Noctem

> Night, that queenest it o'er the ether-born stars,
> Now ruling in the mid-space of heaven,
> Grant pardon if I break thy magical silence with my song !

Sweet love of thee hath drawn me through the shades.
Who can withhold his song from praising thee ?
Who hath not his being burnt clear of earth,
To fuse with thee, made utterly thine ?

Hesper, loved of maidens, gleameth in thy hair,
As a red rose, he gleameth on thy brow.
One is it, if thou makest way to Phœbus' coming,
One if thou sweepest thy hasty garment o'er the sea.
. . . .

With the same dew dost thou scatter
The honey-sweetness upon the violets and growing corn,
And with it thou dost feed
The stars that sanctify thee with their gold-gleaming fires.

In thy hours come forth the nymphs
Who bathe in the cool waters of the ford,
And join in the light dancing line
With their hill-kin Oreads.
Dryads of wood and daughters of the fountains
Sing o'er their chants in mazy circles moving.

Witness thou art of man's love-sorrow,
Cherishing him in the lure of thy shadowy deeps.
Thou restorest his courage when before thy healing doors
Ill-starred he feareth a strange thing and unknown.

Shaggy as is the translation, its substance should prove that
the myths and personifications have for these men a vital
significance.

It is not, however, to Capilupus, but to John Baptist Amaltheus, that we must turn for our finest singing : his *Corydon*,
is typical of the time's taste, both in form and manner.

Corydon

The fields me call again, and the sweet recesses.
The oat-pipe bewitcheth me to compose a field-song,
Close to the water-ways where light wind murmurs
Beneath the willow shade, where waters of Athesis
Flow surrounding.

And even thou, O tribe of heroes, when great Cæsar brought thee
   peace,
Thou, progeny that vied with gods,
Wast wont to make familiar shepherd's haunts
And shadowy hospitalities beneath their trees.
Where the banks are soft the farmers lay their altar gifts,
Set full tables for banqueting,
Poured out new milk, brought fatted lambs ;
Kept up the solemn feasts, lest starry gods grow envious,
For then man's prayers brought man favour.
Wherefore draw nigh, scorn not
The gentler sports of the Muses.
Where Neptune's trident draweth back his towered might,
Corydon leisured ears inciteth.

Happy winds that o'er the dewy sown,
Girdled with Zephyr's gentleness, where spring perennial
Fosters th' eternal flowers and the charmèd green,
Yours the Idalian myrtle. Here the grove stands
Crowned with the Muses' frondage, and Corydon
Sets seven altars here, with green-tipped boughs
Near to the waters of this moss-green fountain.

Make ye soft the heat, and with whispers alluring
Temper the slanted light of th' ardent sun,
Thus : ne'er may cloudy skies make dark your courses
And may the earth and sea both wear for you their smiles.

Now Nisa tendeth my grove
And the wood hears her approaching
Quiver-girded, and the fallow deer swift-flying.
Nor dread'th she the driving of the great stags clamorous.
I envy you, out-breathing winds on the march.
She seeketh the hills, traverseth the inhospitable forests,
An huntress renowned for her bow and the light-flying arrows.
On harsh flanks of wind-worn cliffs, though vast passes
Of the wood gird her round,
Are ye, O winds, her most steadfast companions,
Her fellows in labor.

Over bold she is, alas!
To scour the lonely fields, and she surmounteth
Th' highest peaks of th' unshorn mounts most perilous,
Where grim boar stands to his arms
And wrath and dire lust do drive him monstrous on.

Many a snare is here. Nay! that goddess lacked not in cunning
That erst 'neath Aetna in Sicily gathered her wreaths of new violets,
And was torn unhappy unto that drear realm, the shadow-shrouded,
And there, ill-starred, knew fear of ghosts in Dis the sorrowful,
And hapless drank in terror from flaming streams.
Thou too, reckless Aquillo, vagrant in wayless lands,
Snatched'st Orithyia in thy keen embracing.
O bold Aquillo! turn this wile aside! Here stay thy blast!
But ye, O gentle spirits, dewy-wingèd
That rule in heaven, bear off the unjust heat.

I envy you, O winds, whom Nisa detaineth with subtile song,
To whom her rosy breasts layeth she free,
Whether in the bosom of the pasture lands, or further hidden
In empty cave, where she dreameth alone on our loves, or
Where forests tower up, and all the birds attentive
Stand silent-throated about her and the rivers hush their courses
And she sings,—and heaven laughs all its light.
Now broidereth she the whortle on woven acanthus
And hath pleasure to vary the pattern with snowy lingustris,
Or layeth she bare to calyx slender hibiscus.
Yet if her wearying eyes droop down in sleep,
May ye, O winds, refresh her speedily,
'Gainst heat and weariness and gentle-moving,
Breathe down your shadowy perfumes round about her.

I envy you, O winds, O ye that wander
Through the hospitable glamour of forests and th' unguarded recesses,
And know what hill or vale is Nisa's dwelling.

For rigorous hunts she prepareth her
When Lucifer drencheth the grass in morning dew
And all the fields resound a bird-throat chorus.
Yet ere she treads the grove with bow unbent
She calls her ram to the 'customed feasts of the flowered cythisos.
His horns are bound round with woody garlands and arbutus.

O Ram, so fortunate that none is more so—
Not even he who through the welling seas
Bore Phryxus on his golden back, and gleameth now
Among the fair formed stars—
Adorned art thou with green ivy and amaracus,
And nibbling careless clip'st the meadow-land
Of thy accustomed fields.
'Gainst the whistling winds warm-guarded,
Marvelest at beaten forest's murmuring.

Would that I might slip beneath the wool of thy white back,
Stretch forth the curling horns of thy wide forehead
When night brings Nisa home weighed down with sanguine
    trophies,
And leads thee back to accustomed fold !
Then might she spread for me red-rusted hyacinths and fair-blown
    crocuses
While I pressed stealthy kisses on her maiden hands,
Or butting gleefully might drive her hastening home.

Children of the highest Jove,
You oft with many a prayer I beseech,
And do reverence with the varied gifts of flowers.
Happy winds that round the dewy sown
Are girt about with gentle zephyrs, and with Spring
Perennial feed th' eternal flowers and tend the charmèd sward !

Amaltheus has left us a series of such poems, among them
a *Lycidas*, but the most sincere and passionate elegy which I
have found is by Castiglione. The author of *Il Cortegiano* has
left very few Latin poems, but they are nearly all of interest.
Thus these fragments from the

Alcon

Ta'en of the Fates in the flower of thy years,
Alcon, the grove's glory and the lover's solace,
Whom oft, so oft the fauns and dryads heard singing,
Whom oft, so oft the Sun and Pan admiring have looked on.
Weep now all shepherds.
More than all Iolas whom thou lovedst
Beareth his face most sad with rainèd tears,
Cries down the gods for cruel and the stars for foes.

As, 'mid encircling dark, nightingale
Mourns for her stricken young, and as the widower dove
Mourns for his mate, so I for one
Whom late the oak looked down upon
And found him glad and careless of the morrow.
Him cruel shepherd death with his shrill reed pipeth down.
He knows no more green twigs and rejoicing grass
He drinks no more of the clear stream's sweet current ;
His grove bears witness to the loss of him ;
All withered, its deep recesses are filled with lamenting.
. . . .

Alcon, the muse's joy and Apollo's.
Alcon, our soul's part and our heart's.
Alcon, most greatly ours as grief is now,
Grief that o'erflows our eyes with lasting tears,
What god or what fell doom hath torn thee from us ?

Because ? Because doom's cruelty snatcheth alway the best.
Reaper reaps not the unripe grain,
Yokel plucks not unmellowed fruit,
But wild brute Death pluckth before the day.
. . . .

The fields' joy, love, and the graces, yea, all our light is gone !
The trees put off their pageantries, of honours dishonourèd.
. . . .

With withered grasses the dry fields lay down their glory.

And so it continues :
We that have borne the cold together, we, friends since boyhood,
shall no more lie beneath the oak's shade in summer.
. . . .

If I flee from the long suns of the summer,
Thy pipe shall not fill the surrounding hills with enchantment.

The Poems of Flaminius and the *Idyls* of J. B. Amaltheus are
perhaps the most notable work of this group of writers.

Needless to say, the average work of a pedantic movement

is uninteresting. One must search patiently for beautiful poems embedded in a mass of epistolary poetry and imitations of the classics which are not only slavish but impotent. The writing of epigrams was popular. The results are sometimes graceful, but ninety-nine per cent. at least are unimportant. The following of Hieronimus Angeriani may serve as an illustration :

Ad Rosam

(from the *Erotopægnion*)

Rose of fair form, God grant thee grace !
Thou dost endure but little space ;
Sith old age thou mayst not wear,
Thy time be, as thy face is, fair.

A number of long poems were attempted ; among them one by Marcus Hieronymus Vida, *On the Play of Chess*, beginning :

Let us make game in effigy of war,
Feigning of truth in strife.
Sham battle lines of wood . . .
Let us between two kings, the black and white,
For praise and prizes opposite strive with twi-colored arms.

Aonius Palearius attempted *The Immortality of the Soul* in three books, whereof the first opens :

Happy souls, fosterlings of omnipotent heaven,
Glory of the stars, who on varicolored wings
Swim through the liquid æther and who past the stars
And through the major orbs huge courses turn ;
Since every race of men and beastly species
Sends up its prayers through you, and since through you
Lieth path to luminous coasts,
Ye who bear all things unto the face
Of the great King, ye who are that King's chief care ;
To you the wind-spread sea and castled earth[3]

[3] *Turreta tellus*—towered earth.

Give praise ; the open fields re-sound you
All th' inaccessible forests ring with your voices,
Where there be thickets of brushwood near deep-sounding rivers.
The winged sing sweet to you through the vast void[4]
Ye first showed mortals passage to the stars.

. . . .

By your aid loose I rein for places never trod.

Life is perhaps too short to read either poem in its entirety.
The last lines quoted imply a naïve ignorance of Dante's work,
which the good Palearius would have probably considered
hopelessly Gothic. The pedantry of the Renaissance must have
been insufferable.

Set apart from all the other poetry of the time are those
sonnets which Michael Agnolo seems to have beaten together
with a sculptor's mallet to the glory of Vittoria Colonna, who,
as he says, " hewed his soul from the rock and freed it as the
sculptor the figure from its shrouding."

Buonarroti's poetry is not indicative of any tendency of the
time, except that toward writing poems to Vittoria. None of
the Latinists did it so well as he. To witness, this translation
by J. A. Symonds :

> A man within a woman, nay a God
> Speaks through her spoken word ;
> I therefore who have heard
> Must suffer change, and shall be mine no more.
> She lured me from the paths I whilhom trod,
> Borne from my former state by her away,
> I stand aloof, and mine own self deplore.
> Above all vain desire.
> The beauty of her face doth lift my clay,
> All lesser loveliness seems charnal mire.
> O Lady, who through fire
> And water leadest souls to joy serene,
> Let me no more unto myself return.

[4] Magnum inane.

But Michael Agnolo is against the spirit of the time. He preferred Dante to Bembo. In him survive the Middle Ages ; in a totally different way we find a mediæval quality in the Franciscan temper of Flaminius.

How paganism took possession of art, and how, further, the fashions of praising the gods are adapted to the praising of saints, may be seen from this little prayer of John Carga's :

> *To the Virgin Mother, whose shrine is at Lauretus*
>
> Goddess of the great sea, whose star
> Ruleth the winds twixt shores of ocean,
> For sailors shineth whene'er
> Their prayers stretch sail,
>
>   Calm thou these watery floods of the Adrian
> From thy fostering house at Lauretus, and by thy breath
> Make safe the ships' course, let not Auster
> O'erwhelm us with tempest.
>
> Returned to the ports of our fatherland
> By gifts will we fullfill all vows to thee
> And every shrine along the shore shall flow
> With frankincense and song.

The Cinquecento was a luxurious period ; it wrote copiously. I believe its real gifts to the art of poetry are the two mentioned, the nature feeling and the widening of the scope of the subject matter ; these are, of course, resurrections, not initial contributions. As for the rest, if any modern really enjoys reading, Bembo, Poliziano, Sanazzaro, Ariosto, or even Tasso, let him stand forth and praise them.

One name I have neglected and which is possibly worth mention is that of Aurelius Augurellus. He wrote among other things, *De Poeti*, a short poem, the title of which we may render freely as *Concerning the Artistic Temperament* ; it contains some Ovid, and a certain amount of unintentional humor. He is to be thanked for a fine opening :

Cælestis intus excitat vates vigor
Ultroque semper promonet. . . .

An inward celestial power arouseth the bard and ever moveth him toward the ' beyond.'

His " aegrum vulgus," diseased rabble," is one degree more contemptuous than the " profanum vulgus " of Horace.

Another series of men who are usually neglected in studies of the Renaissance are those whom we might call " The Conservitors," they who fought the long fight in the dark : Cassiodorus, Benedict, St. Columba, Alcuin. Both these and early printers, Aldus, Estienne, Froben of Basel, Plantin, Elzevir of Leyden, The Kobergers, Caxton, who is more familiar, find fitting memorial in Putnam's *Books and their Makers during the Middle Ages*. The vogue of these poets continued in some degree till the French Revolution, and Fracastor was reprinted in or about 1797. Roscoe's *Life of Leo X* contains a certain amount of information regarding them.

Parenthesis 1929 : Tout de même, there was a change in human awareness. Dante's poetic equipment could no more have served to express the emotions of any first-, or even fourth-, rate poet of the Quattro- or Cinquecento than could, let us say, the poetic tool kit of the Oxford '90's express post-war Europe or Paris in the 1920's. (A) there was the new variety of things wanting expression ; (B) there was the difference of attitude. This latter is better studied in the writers of Latin than in the vernacular writers *who got their classicism secondhand via these Latin writers*.

Flaminius' little *Flos tenellus*, or perhaps almost any Renaissance Latin poem will infuriate a classical scholar conscious mainly, or exclusively, of the cribs from the classics ; but take it the other way on. Suppose the reader knows only mediaeval literature and then comes on Renaissance Latin a reader who can imagine such an ignorance for himself may make several discoveries.

In the end we probably come round to the view of the sound classic scholar, but classic scholarship has nevertheless produced or maintained a certain form of ignorance. I mean simply that if a man start with too good a knowledge of Greek and Latin masterwork he seldom has patience enough with mediaeval work to discover what it is all about. He misses the mediaeval values which are, after all, values, and he never understands in the least what the Renaissance was. There are a number of factors and equations which escape him completely.

I had not in 1910 come upon the work of Bassinio. The *Istoteus* probably contains more fine poetry than is to be found in the work of any of the men mentioned in my foregoing essay, and a comparison of Bassinio with Flaminius or Amaltheus would throw a good deal of light on the mental events occurring from 1425 to 1525. The difference between the two centuries, the Fifteenth " of elan, of the new hope," the Sixteenth " of very accomplished performers." All of which takes us a long way from the strict analysis of poetic mechanism proposed in my *How to Read*.

To put it another way : these men can presumably teach us nothing about writing that we couldn't learn better from Homer or Catullus, but they can teach us why Homer and Catullus are today where we can find them ; not merely why there are the editions of Aldus, Stephanus, Clarke, Divus, etc. . . . but why we are in a mental state to receive the text from later editions.

INDEX

INDEX

Some New Directions Paperbooks

Complete descriptive catalog available free on request from
New Directions, 333 Sixth Avenue, New York 10014.   † Bilingual